*A* Map *to the* Door *of*
No Return

# A Map *to the* Door *of* No Return

*Notes to Belonging*

Dionne Brand

VINTAGE CANADA

VINTAGE CANADA EDITION

Published in Canada by Vintage Canada, a division of Penguin Random House
Canada Limited, Toronto. Originally published in hardcover in Canada by Doubleday
Canada, a division of Penguin Random House Canada Limited, Toronto, in 2001.
Distributed by Penguin Random House Canada Limited, Toronto.

Vintage Canada and colophon are registered trademarks.

www.penguinrandomhouse.ca

"Arriving at Desire" appeared in *Desire in Seven Voices*, edited by Lorna Crozier; sections of "Up Here" were previously published in *Toronto Life*.

**Library and Archives Canada Cataloguing in Publication**

Brand, Dionne, 1953–
    A map to the door of no return : notes to belonging / Dionne Brand

ISBN 978-0-385-25892-0

1. Brand, Dionne, 1953–    2. Authors, Canadian (English)—20TH
century—Biography.  3. Blacks—Canada—Race identity.  4. Blacks—Canada—
Social conditions. I. Title.

PS855.3R275Z53 2002    C818'.5409    C2002-902620-2
PR9199.3B683Z47 2002

Cover image: Detail from Willem Blaeu's "Africa Newly Described,"
courtesy Steve Luck/Tooley, Adams & Co., UK
Cover design by Leah Springate

Printed and bound in Canada

9

 Penguin
Random House
VINTAGE CANADA

*Dedicated*
*to the other dwellers of the door*

*There are maps to the Door of No Return. The physical door. They are well worn, gone over by cartographer after cartographer, refined from Ptolemy's Geographia to orbital photographs and magnetic field imaging satellites. But to the Door of No Return which is illuminated in the consciousness of Blacks in the Diaspora there are no maps. This door is not mere physicality. It is a spiritual location. It is also perhaps a psychic destination. Since leaving was never voluntary, return was, and still may be, an intention, however deeply buried. There is as it says no way in; no return.*

*A Circumstantial Account of a State of Things*

My grandfather said he knew what people we came from. I reeled off all the names I knew. Yoruba? Ibo? Ashanti? Mandingo? He said no to all of them, saying that he would know it if he heard it. I was thirteen. I was anxious for him to remember.

I pestered him for days. He told me to stop bothering him and that he would remember. Or stop bothering or else he would not remember. I hovered about him in any room in which he rested. I followed him around asking him if he wanted me to do this or that for him, clean his glasses, polish his shoes, bring his tea. I studied him intently when he came home. I searched the grey bristles of his moustache for any flicker which might suggest he was about to speak. He raised his *Sunday Guardian* newspaper to block my view. He shooed me away, telling me to find some book to read or work to do. At times it seemed as if Papa was on the brink of remembering. I imagined pulling the word off his tongue if only I knew the first syllable.

I scoured the San Fernando library and found no other lists of names at the time. Having no way of finding other names, I could only repeat the ones I knew, asking him if he was sure it wasn't Yoruba, how about Ashanti? I couldn't help myself. I wanted to be either one. I had heard that they were noble people. But I could also be Ibo; I had heard that they were gentle. And I had followed the war in Biafra. I was on their side.

Papa never remembered. Each week he came I asked him had he remembered. Each week he told me no. Then I stopped asking. He was disappointed. I was disappointed. We lived after that in this mutual disappointment. It was a rift between us. It gathered into a kind of estrangement. After that he grew old. I grew young. A small space opened in me.

I carried this space with me. Over time it has changed shape and light as the question it evoked has changed in appearance and angle. The name of the people we came from has ceased to matter. A name would have comforted a thirteen-year-old. The question however was more complicated, more nuanced. That moment between my grandfather and I several decades ago revealed a tear in the world. A steady answer would have mended this fault line quickly. I would have proceeded happily with a simple name. I may have played with it for a few days and then stored it away.

Forgotten. But the rupture this exchange with my grandfather revealed was greater than the need for familial bonds. It was a rupture in history, a rupture in the quality of being. It was also a physical rupture, a rupture of geography.

My grandfather and I recognized this, which is why we were mutually disappointed. And which is why he could not lie to me. It would have been very easy to confirm any of the names I'd proposed to him. But he could not do this because he too faced this moment of rupture. We were not from the place where we lived and we could not remember where we were from or who we were. My grandfather could not summon up a vision of landscape or a people which would add up to a name. And it was profoundly disturbing.

Having no name to call on was having no past; having no past pointed to the fissure between the past and the present. That fissure is represented in the Door of No Return: that place where our ancestors departed one world for another; the Old World for the New. The place where all names were forgotten and all beginnings recast. In some desolate sense it was the creation place of Blacks in the New World Diaspora at the same time that it signified the end of traceable beginnings. Beginnings that can be noted through a name or a set of family stories that extend farther into the past than five hundred or so years, or the kinds of beginnings that can be expressed in a name which in turn marked out territory or occupation. I am interested in exploring this creation place — the Door of No Return, a place emptied of beginnings — as a site of belonging or unbelonging.

## Maps

The rufous hummingbird travels five thousand miles from summer home to winter home and back. This humming-bird can fit into the palm of a hand. Its body defies the known physics of energy and flight. It knew its way before all known map-makers. It is a bird whose origins and paths are the blood of its small body. It is a bird whose desire to find its way depends on drops of nectar from flowers.

## Water

Water is the first thing in my imagination. Over the reaches of the eyes at Guaya when I was a little girl, I knew that there was still more water. All beginning in water, all ending in water. Turquoise, aquamarine, deep green, deep blue, ink blue, navy, blue-black cerulean water.

To the south of this island on a clear day you could see the mainland of South America. Women and men with a tinge of red in the black of their faces and a burnt copper to their hair would arrive from the mainland to this island fleeing husbands or the law, or fleeing life. To the north was the hinterland of Trinidad, leading to the city which someone with great ambition in another century called Port-of-Spain. To the west was the bird's beak of Venezuela and to the east, the immense Atlantic gaping to Africa.

The sea behind the house where I was born was a rough country sea, with a long wide shining white beach. I recall waking up each day to discover what it had brought us, and what it had carried away. The word *gaze* only applies to water. To look into this water was to look into the world, or what I thought was the world, because the sea gave one an immediate sense of how large the world was, how magnificent and how terrifying. The sea was its own country, its own sovereignty. There was always some uncontrollable news from it. Either it had taken a fisherman or it was about to wash a house away. It was either taking a child or would take a child. To take a child away. That type of away was the most fearsome news. The sea was feared and loved, generous to a fault. Boats laden with kingfish, red snapper, lobster, and bonito came in with a fisherman who had cut his foot on a fatal coral. Logs and stone which once were churches, sand which once was human, or animal bones arrived on surprising tides. "Never turn your back on the ocean," was the counsel.

Water is the first thing in my memory. The sea sounded like a thousand secrets, all whispered at the same time. In the daytime it was indistinguishable to me from air. It seemed to be made of the same substance. The same substance which carried voices or smells, music or emotion. The water misted the air in a continuous fine spray. It insulated the place where we lived so much so that when you entered Guaya from the bend in the Mayaro Road it felt like a surprise. A quiet, peaceful surprise.

Right there at the bend, the sea sighed as at the end of a long journey. Guayguayare is where the sea came to rest. You would not know that there in that place there were fierce quarrels and illicit romances. You would not know that old age did not limit your sexual encounters or seductions; I know this from the hushed whispers of my grandfather's infidelities. You would not know that runaway madmen lived there; I know this from the madman who so loved my grandfather he came to the door at night, his voice disguised as a woman, calling. You would not know there were men who fathered their daughters' children; I know this about the man named

Sonny who lived in the estate workers' barracks, fathering the children of his wife and daughters simultaneously. Sonny was the only one happy there. His wife and daughters always seemed washed with dread and exhaustion.

You would probably go past the small shop owned by Miss Jeanne and think the bottles of dinner mints and sweet plums dull. You would not know how dazzling they were on a Sunday to a girl in black patent-leather shoes and a pink dress stiffened with starch and pressed to perfection by a doting aunt. The perfume of roasting bakes and smoked herring lulls anyone into a thing like paradise; the sea and the bush multiplied a laugh into daylong echoes; and early morning smoke and mist could muffle the screams of children pleading not to be washed or combed. A braying donkey can be heard as if from far away, a horse's sneeze, a high-pitched threatening calling from everywhere, in men's voices, women's voices — a harsh ululation which was the waking-up sound of this place some mornings. As if one had to be cruel to approach the coming day, or be hard at least. But whatever human din and rumble, whatever unhappinesses or raptures, the sea took it in and flung it back like nothing.

It's difficult to live near the sea. It overwhelms. Well, not true. It owns. Your small life is nothing to it. The sea uses everything. Small things like bits of black bottles and rusty bottle tops, smoothed transparent fish, fish bone, cockles against small rocks. New houses poised in concrete at its mouth could end up kilometres away days later. The sea can make a tree into spongy bits, it can wear away a button to a shell. It can wash away blood and heal wounds.

When I was small this is what I noticed. One day two men got into a fight on the beach at Guaya. They parried glistening, sharpened cutlasses. Their faces were chiselled and murderous. I cannot recall what the fight was about. I could not know anyway. People tried to part them, their wives and their friends, but they were relentless. In the end, people gave up and left them to murder each other. In their rage one man raised his cutlass high to lay it on the other's neck; the other slipped quickly sideways, slicing his own weapon through the muscle of the man's arm. A seam of blood opened over a long flap of flesh from shoulder to wrist, exposing for a moment bloodless white fat. The man looked down at his arm; the other ran toward land. Then the man with the bloody, limp arm fled for the sea, his cutlass still hanging from his other arm. The sea took his blood. He tried to cauterize the wound with the sea's salt; the sea became pink. I saw him standing there still enraged, his flesh wide open and the green wave with its swatch of pink steaming toward the beach. It wasn't over. In a small place nothing is ever over.

People here believe in uncontrollable passion, in mad rages, and in the brusque inevitability of death. Or damage. As if a face would not be a face without a scar, a finger not a finger without being broken, or a foot not a foot without a limp. Or a life not a life without tragedy. These things I knew before I knew they had something to do with the Door of No Return and the sea. I knew that everyone here was unhappy and haunted in some way. Life spoke in the blunt language of brutality, even beauty was brutal. I did not know what we were haunted by at the time. Or why it would be imperfect to have a smooth face, or why a moment of hatred would take hold so easily as if the sun had simply come out. But I had a visceral understanding of a wound much deeper than the physical, a wound which somehow erupted in profound self-disappointment, self-hatred, and disaffection. Someday the man with the bloody seam in his arm would catch the other man and do him the same harm. This I saw when I was small.

The sea would forever be larger than me. My eyes hit only its waist. I saw a wave's belly looking backwards, I saw froth rolling toward my feet as the sea moved into my spot on the beach. It always came in a jagged circle, frothing and steaming. It reduced all life to its unimportant random meaning. Only we were changing and struggling, living as if everything was urgent, feeling — the ocean was bigger than feeling. It lay at the back of us, on the borders of quarrels and disagreements. It took our happiness as minor and transitory. My family was large and unwieldy, and then it also contained far cousins, and friends so old they shared the same skin and blood. In that place anyone could tell your family by the mere tracing of your hairline or tilt of your head or by the way you walked. How we ended up there in a place my family jokingly called "quite to quite" is unknown to me. Our origins seemed to be in the sea. It had brought the whole of Guayguayare there from unknown places, unknown origins. Unknown to me at the time and even more unknown now.

My grandfather, who knew everything, had forgotten, as if it was not worth remembering, the name of our tribe in that deeply unknown place before the trade. Derek Walcott wrote, "the sea is history." I knew that before I knew it was history I was looking at.

## Maps

According to *Cosmas Indicopleustes Topographia Christiana* the world was an oblong shaped like the tabernacle Moses built. Beyond the earth lay Paradise, which was the source of four rivers that watered the earth.

*In a blue while*

At eight in the morning the radio in the living room crackles
over the gulls and roosters and then there is a sound like the
sound of a shell with your ear in it and in the middle is the
ovular sound of the BBC. It is the news from away. Once in
a while an island is mentioned, once in a blue while.

You hear that you are living elsewhere. The BBC announcer
is calling you. Telling you the news. Elsewhere is not a bad
place at all. It is simply elsewhere. You have heard it described
as an island. You have read of islands, such as in the *Tempest*
described as uninhabited except for monsters and spirits, as
in *Treasure Island* described as uninhabited except for
monsters and spirits; you have read of pirates and buccaneers
on islands; you have read of people banished to islands, prisoners. You have seen on the borders of maps of islands,
natives, nubile and fierce. You are living on an island,
banished or uninhabited, or so it seems through the voice of
the BBC. You are therefore already mythic.

A long strip of sun-scarred beach, an anticipation of natives,
pleasant or unpleasant, a full unending gasp of water called
ocean or the savage sea which has shipwrecked you on this
island, and which is the barrier between you and civilization. Since it is myth, time does not mark this island, nor

progress, except that which you may fashion out of its primitive tools. It is otherwise unchanging. And you, your ear against the radio again at four in the afternoon, the living room crackling and humming with more news from away, you listening.

The news of the BBC is a door to "over there," it is the door to being in the big world. Your grandfather positions the radio so that the sea's spray does not rust out the wires. He twists and turns the aerial for cleaner reception. Your grandmother and grandfather silence all when the BBC is on. They too are shipwrecked and waiting for news of rescue. Something important is about to be said. A hush falls over the living room, the front door is closed. The neighbours who have no radio are shut out. Gamal Abdel Nasser is dead . . . Mahatma Gandhi is fasting . . . Lady Baden Powell is to visit the islands, the Suez Canal is to be opened . . . President Charles de Gaulle is to visit England on a state visit . . . Generalissimo Franco has declared martial law . . . President John F. Kennedy has been shot in Dallas, Texas . . . The plane carrying Patrice Lumumba has crashed . . . The war in Biafra has escalated . . . The writer V.S. Naipaul has received the Booker Prize . . . The queen has knighted . . . The cricketer . . . Dieppe commemoration . . . In Flanders field we shall not sleep till poppies grow . . .

The world kept coming. We listened. Year in, year out. Except for Sundays. There were no BBC broadcasts on Sundays. Sundays, the island was the island; the island was itself, quiet, cicadas signalling across fields. Sun absorbing everything into light, sleep blessing the eyes after lunch at two o'clock; or the rain dipping the island grey, drenching it into the same silence. I found Sundays boring. I could not wait for them to pass to listen again to the world outside. To feel the strange intimacy of coveted estrangement, of envied cosmopolitanism.

The time between the BBC at eight and the BBC at four was filled with brown school uniforms and lessons in the proper use of English; the proper use of knives and forks, the proper use of pens and inkwells, and the proper use of leather straps; the proper use of speech; the proper use of everything. Once per year at Christmas the island entered the world when families listened for greetings from sons, daughters, cousins, sisters, and mothers abroad, broadcast by the BBC. "Hello Ma, Pa, Eddie, Mitzie, all the children and friends . . ." "Hello Ma, Pa, Daddy, and Granny . . . wishing I was there with you at these holidays . . ." "Hello Ma, Pa . . ." "Hello Ma, Pappy. Roland, I hope you are being a good boy. Edna, your mommy loves you. Special greetings to Auntie Doris, uncle Dan, and cousin Tee; may God bless and keep you safe." The whole island pressed its ear against the radio, listening for itself.

## Maps

A Babylonian map circa 500 BC shows a disc representing the earth. Around it is the "Bitter River" or ocean, then beyond that are triangles representing "hazards" — "places where a horned bull lurks, perhaps, or where it is always twilight." Where it is always twilight.

## Forgetting

David Turnbull writes in *Maps Are Territories*, "In Order to find our way successfully, it is not enough just to have a map. We need a cognitive schema as well as practical mastery of way-finding."

In order to find our way successfully . . .

### 1

My grandfather never remembered our name and perhaps therefore, in a large sense for me, our way. I balanced on the word at the tip of his tongue. He left me in this anticipation and therefore curiosity. For the name he could not remember was from the place we could not remember. Africa. It was the place we did not remember, yet it lodged itself in all the conversations of who we were. It was a visible secret. Through the BBC broadcasts we were inhabited by British consciousness. We were also inhabited by an unknown self. The African. This duality was fought every day from the time one woke up to the time one fell asleep. As we went out to be schooled in Englishness and as we returned home to say Christian prayers in the evenings. One had the sense that some being had to be erased and some being had to be cultivated. Even our dreams were not free of this conflict. We floated on an imaginary island imagining a "Dark Continent." That "Dark Continent" was a source of denial and awkward embrace. The African self so abiding yet so fearful because it was informed by colonial images of the African as savage and not by anything we could call on our memories to conjure. No amount of denial, however, dislodged this place, this self, and no amount of forgetting obscured the Door of No Return.

2

Wishing to search for this door I have sought out a book of maps: Charles Bricker's text to *Landmarks of Mapmaking: An Illustrated Survey of Maps and Mapmakers chosen and displayed by R. V. Tooley.* In this book of the history of maps, places mature from landlocked water to open seas. The coastlines of "new territories" are peppered with forts and settlements, the interior is filled with dread and imagined riches. Explorers, sailing along the coast, called what they did not or could not see deep and dark, moving inland little by little toward their own fears.

Bricker notes, "Ludolf, the 17th century German founder of Ethiopian studies, never visited Abyssinia — but relying on the reports of Portuguese missionaries like Father Lobo he constructed a new map of the region in 1683." Without ever having visited himself. Which proves to me something of which I've had a nagging inkling — that places and those who inhabit them are indeed fictions. This news has cemented the idea that in order to draw a map only the skill of listening may be necessary. And the mystery of interpretation.

This skill, this mystery eluded my grandfather and me. The Door of No Return is of course no place at all but a metaphor for place. Ironically, or perhaps suitably, it is no one place but a collection of places. Landfalls in Africa, where a castle was built, a house for slaves, *une maison des esclaves*. Rude enough to disappear or elaborate and vain enough to survive after centuries. A place where a certain set of transactions occurred, perhaps the most important of them being the transference of selves. The Door of No Return — real and metaphoric as some places are, mythic to those of us scattered in the Americas today. To have one's belonging lodged in a metaphor is voluptuous intrigue; to inhabit a trope; to be a kind of fiction. To live in the Black Diaspora is I think to live as a fiction — a creation of empires, and also self-creation. It is to be a being living inside and outside of herself. It is to apprehend the sign one makes yet to be unable to escape it except in radiant moments of ordinariness made like art. To be a fiction in search of its most resonant metaphor then is even more intriguing. So I am scouring maps of all kinds, the way that some fictions do, discursively, elliptically, trying to locate their own transferred selves.

So far I've collected these fragments, like Ludolf — disparate and sometimes only related by sound or intuition, vision or aesthetic. I have not visited the Door of No Return, but by relying on random shards of history and unwritten memoir of descendants of those who passed through it, including me, I am constructing a map of the region, paying attention to faces, to the unknowable, to unintended acts of returning, to impressions of doorways. Any act of recollection is important, even looks of dismay and discomfort. Any wisp of a dream is evidence.

### 3

The door is a place, real, imaginary and imagined. As islands and dark continents are. It is a place which exists or existed. The door out of which Africans were captured, loaded onto ships heading for the New World. It was the door of a million exits multiplied. It is a door many of us wish never existed. It is a door which makes the word *door* impossible and dangerous, cunning and disagreeable.

There is the sense in the mind of not being here or there, of no way out or in. As if the door had set up its own reflection. Caught between the two we live in the Diaspora, in the sea in between. Imagining our ancestors stepping through these portals one senses people stepping out into nothing; one senses a surreal space, an inexplicable space. One imagines people so stunned by their circumstances, so heartbroken as to refuse reality. Our inheritance in the Diaspora is to live in this inexplicable space. That space is the measure of our ancestors' step through the door toward the ship. One is caught in the few feet in between. The frame of the doorway is the only space of true existence.

Castles and forts, the most famous being St. George d'Elmina and the Cape Coast Castle, peppered the coast of West Africa for such purposes from the 1600s to the end of the trade. From Elmina in 1700, William Bosman, the Dutch chief factor dealing in gold and slaves, wrote in his letters home, adoringly, ". . . for to speak but the bare truth of it, for beauty and strength it hath not its equal upon the coast." All of those castles, their strong doors leading to ships, have collected in the imagination as the Door of No Return. Elmina sits there still. Whitewashed over the sea. There is a fishing village below. The harbour is filled with colourful boats. I've seen photographs.

For those of us today in the Diaspora this door exists as through a prism, distorted and shimmering. As through heat waves across a vast empty space we see this door appearing and disappearing. An absent presence. Though few of us have seen it, or consciously attach importance to it, this door in its historical connectedness was the point of departure, not only physical departure but psychic renting, of our ancestors.

Leaving? To leave? Left? Language can be deceptive. The moment when they "left" the Old World and entered the New. Forced to leave? To "leave" one would have to have a destination in mind. Of course one could rush out of a door with no destination in mind, but "to rush" or "to leave" would suggest some self-possession; rushing would suggest a purpose, a purpose with some urgency, some reason. Their "taking"? Taking, taking too might suggest a benevolence so, no, it was not taking. So having not "left," having no "destination," having no "self-possession," no purpose and no urgency, their departure was unexpected; and in the way that some unexpected events can be horrific, their "leaving," or rather their "taking," was horrific. What language would describe that loss of bearings or the sudden awful liability of one's own body? The hitting or the whipping or the driving, which was shocking, the dragging and the bruising it involved, the epidemic sickness with life which would become hereditary? And the antipathy which would shadow all subsequent events.

The door looms both as a horror and a romance, though. The horror is of course three or four hundred years of slavery, its shadow was and is colonialism and racism. The romance is of the place beyond the door, the Africa of our origins. Some of us reinvent these origins as a golden past of serenity, grandeur, equality — as one living in a state of dread invents its opposite for sustenance. Invention aside, any past without slavery would be golden. Some would simply like the relief of its existence, its continuity rather, its simple connection as a touchstone to our present. This door is the place of the fall.

4

*When these Slaves come to Fida, they are put in Prison all together, and when we treat concerning buying them, they are all brought out together in a large Plain; where, by our Chirurgeons, whose Province it is, they are thoroughly examined, even to the smallest Member, and that naked too both Men and Women, without the least Distinction or Modesty. Those which are approved as good are set on one side; and the lame or faulty are set by as Invalides, which are here called Mackrons.*

*. . . When we have agreed with the Owners of the Slaves, they are returned to their Prison; where from that time forwards they are kept at our charge, cost us two pence a day a Slave; which serves to subsist them, like our Criminals, on Bread and Water: So that to save*

*Charges we send them on Board our Ships with the very first Opportunity; before which their Masters strip them of all they have on their Backs; so that they come Aboard stark-naked as well Women as Men: In which condition they are obliged to continue, if the Master of the Ship is not so Charitable (which he commonly is) as to bestow something on them to cover their Nakedness.*

*You would really wonder to see how these Slaves live on Board; for though their number sometimes amounts to six or seven Hundred, yet by the careful Management of our Masters of Ships, they are so regulated that it seems incredible: And in this particular our Nation exceeds all other Europeans; for as the French, Portuguese and English Slave-Ships, are always foul and stinking; on the contrary ours are for the most part clean and neat.*

*. . . We are sometimes sufficiently plagued with a parcel of Slaves, which come from a far In-land Country, who very innocently perswade one another, that we buy them only to fatten and afterwards eat them as a Delicacy.*

*When we are so unhappy as to be pestered with many of this sort, they resolve and agree together (and bring over the rest to their Party) to run away from the Ship, kill the Europeans, and set the Vessel a-shore; by*

*which means they design to free themselves from being*
*our Food.*

*I have twice met with this Misfortune; and the first*
*time proved very unlucky to me, I not in the least*
*suspecting it; but the Up-roar was timely quashed by*
*the Master of the Ship and my self, by causing the*
*Abettor to be shot through the Head, after which all*
*was quiet.*

— Letter, William Bosman, 1700

## 5

Migration. Can it be called migration? There is a sense of
return in migrations — a sense of continuities, remembered
homes — as with birds or butterflies or deer or fish. Those
returns which are lodged indelibly, unconsciously, instinc-
tively in the mind. But migrations suggest intentions or
purposes. Some choice and, if not choice, decisions. And if
not decisions, options, all be they difficult. But the sense of
return in the Door of No Return is one of irrecoverable losses
of those very things which make returning possible. A place
to return to, a way of being, familiar sights or sounds, familiar smells, a welcome perhaps, but a place, welcome or not.

## 6

The door signifies the historical moment which colours all
moments in the Diaspora. It accounts for the ways we

observe and are observed as people, whether it's through the lens of social injustice or the lens of human accomplishments. The door exists as an absence. A thing in fact which we do not know about, a place we do not know. Yet it exists as the ground we walk. Every gesture our bodies make somehow gestures toward this door. What interests me primarily is probing the Door of No Return as consciousness. The door casts a haunting spell on personal and collective consciousness in the Diaspora. Black experience in any modern city or town in the Americas is a haunting. One enters a room and history follows; one enters a room and history precedes. History is already seated in the chair in the empty room when one arrives. Where one stands in a society seems always related to this historical experience. Where one can be observed is relative to that history. All human effort seems to emanate from this door. How do I know this? Only by self-observation, only by looking. Only by feeling. Only by being a part, sitting in the room with history.

7

Very few family stories, few personal stories have survived among the millions of descendants of the trade. Africa is therefore a place strictly of the imagination — what is imagined therefore is a gauzy, elliptical, generalized, vague narrative of a place. Many in the Diaspora have visited the Door of No Return at slave castles in Ghana or Gorée Island. They tell of the overwhelming sense of grief and pain these visits give. One does not return to the Diaspora with good news from the door except the news that it exists and that its existence is the truth. Its perpetual "no" denies them relief, denies an ending or reconciliation. Some have recorded a sense of familiarity beyond the door; some have spoken of a welcome, or of no welcome. But their grief, our grief, remains unassuageable at a profound level. No seeing can truly verify the door, no real place can actualize the lost place. Not in any personal sense.

## 8

Flung out and dispersed in the Diaspora, one has a sense of being touched by or glimpsed from this door. As if walking down a street someone touches you on the shoulder but when you look around there is no one, yet the air is oddly warm with some live presence. That touch is full of ambivalence; it is partly comforting but mostly discomforting, tortured, burning with angered, unknowable remembrance. More disturbing, it does not confine itself to remembrance; you look around you and present embraces are equally discomforting, present glimpses are equally hostile. Art, perhaps music, perhaps poetry, perhaps stories, perhaps aching constant movement — dance and speed — are the only comforts. *Being* in the Diaspora braces itself in virtuosity or despair.

# 9

One has this sense as one observes bodies in the Diaspora, virtuosity or despair, on the brink of both.

A body pushing a grocery cart through the city housing at Lawrence and Bathurst in Toronto, her laundry, her shopping all contained there, dressed as if on her way to a party, gold chain around her neck, lipstick — as if moving with all her possessions. Young, perhaps a mother, the cart trundling farther away from the supermarket than it ought to go.

Or someone equally young at a bus stop outside a university explaining some theory of pan-Africanism in which polygamy is the authentic family structure. And how it was, he says, back in Africa before we were brought here. He has an earring in his left ear, his lips curl in superiority. His companion is a young woman who looks at him skeptically yet uneasily, as if she knows that she will have to give in to the argument for the sake of the coming romance.

And another body making its way through a second-hand bookstore looking for Nabakov's *Lolita*; imagining himself this mix of sophistication, taste, and dark passion. He stands reading in the store, the smell of paper, crumpled, dusty, curled around him, the quiet of the shelves buffering the street noise up the stairs and outside, and the sweat of his disturbing presence if he climbs the stairs and goes into the street, unhappily, still himself.

Still another, her mind on the odd lyric to a love song as she burns hair in a beauty salon, the rows of permed wet hair waiting to be blown dry, the Saturday still too early to think of going home, the love song about how good someone promises to make love to her.

Yet another is heading straight to the library to crack her head on Kristeva and Spivak before she sits before a committee that will always be present to her as she makes her way grudgingly and insecurely through academia, through life, never sure, always sure that she is never in control.

That one, a boy still, limbs longer than he can handle, eyes more shy than he wants to reveal. He'll be shocked into hardness any second now, just out of his mother's reach, her hand oiling his face. He'll know in a minute what's expected; she'll know by and by. Their two paths are virtuosity and despair.

## 10

"We need a cognitive schema . . ." This door is really the door of dreams. This existence in the Diaspora is like that — dreams from which one never wakes. Then what here can be called cognition let alone a schema? A set of dreams, a strand of stories which never come into being, which never coalesce. One is not in control in dreams; dreams take place, the dreamer is captive, even though it is the dreamer who is dreaming. Captured in one's own body, in one's own thoughts, to be out of possession of one's mind; our cognitive schema is captivity. But what of all rebellions, emancipations, political struggles for human rights? Aren't these part of the schema, too? Yes. Except for the perpetual retreats and recoveries. In the Diaspora, as in bad dreams, you are constantly overwhelmed by the persistence of the spectre of captivity. The door of dreams.

## Maps

### I

All the days of my life I have seen nothing that rejoiced my heart so much as these things, for I saw amongst them wonderful works of art, and I marveled at the subtle Ingenia of people in foreign lands.

Albrecht Durer, 1519,
when he saw artifacts that had been sent, together with six
Aztecs, by Hernan Cotes to Charles V

## II

Katherina alt 20 jar: "I have drawn the portrait in charcoal of Faktor Brandao's Secretary. I drew a portrait of his negress with metal point." Katherina was the servant of a Portuguese factor, Joao Brandao. The Portuguese at the time controlled the shipping routes to Asia and Africa. Katherina was African, enslaved. Durer was also a collector of exotica: parrots, tortoises, monkeys, Chinese porcelains, African ivories, coral, cane arrows, fish skins, buffalo horns, coconuts.

All artists are involved in their time.

*Captive and Inhabited*

## I

### 1

Those men, raiding villages, leading coffles, throwing buckets of water, those examining limbs and teeth, those looking into eyes for rebellion, those are the captors who enter the captive's body. Already inhabiting them as extensions of themselves with a curious dissociation which gave them the ability to harm them as well. Slaves became extensions of slave owners — their arms, legs, the parts of them they wished to harness and use with none of the usual care of their own bodies. These captive bodies represent parts of their own bodies that they wish to rationalize or make mechanical or inhuman so as to perform the tasks of exploitation of resources or acquisition of territory. These captive bodies then become the tools sent out to conquer the natural world. Of course they aren't merely tools but the projections of the sensibilities, consciousness, needs, desires, and fears of the captor.

## 2

Henry Louis Gates sits across from a man in Kumasi. He has come to Africa to film a PBS scene about African civilization, the Middle Passage, the Door of No Return; the connections between the Diaspora and the continent. The man across from him is Black; he might be a descendant of a slave trader, as he is a descendant of a prominent family in Kumasi, and Kumasi was a major trading centre for slaves. I expect an intelligent, dispassionate discussion about the geopolitics of the time. Suddenly a plaintive and childish question from Henry Louis Gates: to paraphrase, "Why did you sell us?" The Kumasi man of course has no answer. His look is sheepish — as if he is implicated in the present. Gates, a usually sophisticated erudite, is completely genuine, as if addressing a brother or an uncle or a cousin. Nothing matters, not the geopolitics, not political history, not colonialism, not all the time in between. Gates picks up after centuries as if they had spoken only days or months or even just a few years ago; as if he knew this man and had simply been waiting until he saw him in person to ask him, "Why did you sell us?" I switch the station, suddenly embarrassed at the question and the answer. There is no answer. The Door of No Return is ajar between them. I can see its impossibility. They are as in an old remembered attitude. Gates, in all his other explorations of the continent, is the quintessential American traveller, oohing and ahing about wonders, skeptical about claims of civilization, lecturing about civilization, fearful about being in Africa, revelling in the occasional familiarity and pointing out dissimilarity wisely. But here, faced at last with the man from Kumasi, he asks a childlike question to which there is no answer.

3

*Not a few in our Country fondly imagine that Parents here sell their Children, Men their Wives, and one Brother the other: But those who think so deceive themselves; for this never happens on any other account but that of Necessity, or some great Crime: But most of the Slaves that are offered to us are Prisoners of War, which are sold by the Victors as their Booty.*

*. . . But yet before we can deal with any Person, we*

*are obliged to buy the King's whole stock of Slaves at a set price; which is commonly one third or one fourth higher than ordinary: After which we obtain free leave to deal with all his Subjects of what Rand soever. But if there happen to be no stock of Slaves, the Factor must then resolve to run the risk of trusting the Inhabitants with Goods to the value of one or two hundred Slaves; which Commodities they send into the In-land Country, in order to buy with them Slaves at all Markets, and that sometimes two hundred miles deep in the Country: For you ought to be informed that Markets of Men are here kept in the same manner as those of beasts with us.*

— Letter, William Bosman, 1700

In another portion of the documentary, Gates brings several African-Americans to the Door of No Return — a slave castle in Ghana, Elmina. They stand or sit in various states of emotional collapse as Gates probes them on whether they know that their ancestors were sold by Africans. They reply no. The knowledge seems to add greater sadness to them. The scene is full of silences. Even a film editor cannot cut out or put in such silences.

## 4

More than two hundred years ago a strange variation of Gates's conversation with the man from Kumasi took place between a man captured into slavery and the British explorer Mungo Park.

*As I was one day conversing with the slaves which this Slatee had brought, one of them begged me to give him some victuals. I told him I was a stranger, and had none to give. He replied, "I gave you victuals when you was hungry. Have you forgot the man who bought you milk at Karankalla? But (added he, with a sigh) the irons were not then upon my legs!" immediately recollected him, and begged some ground nuts from Karfa to give him, as a return for his former kindness. He told me that he had been taken by the Bambarrans, the day after the battle at Joka, and sent to Sego; where he had been purchased by his master, who was carrying him down to Kajaaga.*

## 5

"It is not enough just to have a map. We need a cognitive schema . . ." What if the cognitive schema is captivity? Then Gates can only ask his question, his question without expecting an answer, because it is a question, really, of the heart. Surely the intelligence of the heart knows there is no answer worth hearing, no answer able to salve its breakage. No answer is forgivable and forgiveness, to tell the truth, will not do.

## II

### 1

The body is the place of captivity. The Black body is situated as a sign of particular cultural and political meanings in the Diaspora. All of these meanings return to the Door of No Return — as if those leaping bodies, those prostrate bodies, those bodies made to dance and then to work, those bodies curdling under the singing of whips, those bodies cursed, those bodies valued, those bodies remain curved in these attitudes. They remain fixed in the ether of history. They leap onto the backs of the contemporary — they cleave not only to the collective and acquired memories of their descendants but also to the collective and acquired memories of the other. We all enter those bodies.

The Black body is a domesticated space as much as it is a wild space. It is domesticated in the sense that there are set characteristics ascribed to the body which have the effect of familiarizing people with it — making it a kind of irrefutable common sense or knowledge. It is a wild space in the sense that it is a sign of transgression, opposition, resistance, and desire. The Black body is culturally encoded as physical prowess, sexual fantasy, moral transgression, violence, magical musical artistry. These ascriptions are easily at hand for everyday use. Much as one would use a tool or instrument to execute some need or want.

2

The Black body is a kind of "naturalized" body in the popular culture. Appreciated in athletes, musicians, singers; absent in the public discourse as associated with the scientific — the scientific being the remaining range of activity, activity having formal authority. In Western culture the natural is always captive to science. When unappreciated, the Black body is shown walking, single file or double chained, in film footage of prisoners in bright orange overalls or in prison boot camps as young offenders, or in sweeping shots along barred prison interiors which strangely, filmed in colour, look like black-and-white film. So dominant are these images, so compelling, that their affectations have been adopted by young people who wear baggy trousers which hobble their feet into the shuffle of chained prisoners in ill-sized clothing. Other styles of captivity have also been adopted, such as the one-legged trouser hitched to the knees, not to mention of course the multinationals like Benetton whose ad campaign featured prisoners on death row, a good many of whom were Black. The many permutations and inversions of the original captivity leach into the contemporary popular discourse and the common sense. These captives, the contemporary young people in orange overalls, give off the essence of danger, of emotions out of control which have to be suppressed, of a violence, if not put under control, which will come down like a flood on the whole of society. Most of these young people are incarcerated for drug use or petty drug dealing, and one cannot miss the scowling presences these images cast, nor the code they transmit.

In many senses the Black body is one of the most regulated bodies in the Diaspora. Perhaps the most regulated body is the female body, any female body, but the Black body is a close and symbolic second. (The female body is also a "naturalized" body — like the Black body having no ability to articulate itself outside of its given "natural" functions. It too is a domesticated space, a space taken over by a process, cultivated into a symbol.) By regulated I mean that there are specific societal functions which it is put to, quite outside of its own agency — functions which in fact deny and resist its agency. It is as if its first appearance through the Door of No Return, dressed in its new habit of captive and therefore slave, is embedded in all its subsequent and contemporary appearances.

## 3

The Black body is signed as physically and psychically open space, almost always in the Diaspora. A space not simply owned by those who embody it but constructed and occupied by other embodiments. Inhabiting it is a domestic, hemispheric pastime, a transatlantic pastime, an international pastime. There is a playing around in it. There is marvel at its strength or grace or speed or agility. As well, there is a constant manipulation of its transgressive trope. More than marvel, of course, there is the not unwilling commercial exploitation of the Black body.

I hear my neighbour downstairs enter Shaquille O'Neal's body every night of the NBA championships this year, 2000. He, my neighbour, is white, I don't know of what origin. I have glimpsed him sometimes — average height, average weight, thirtysomething. We fight, he and I, over his noisy bathroom fan, which he keeps on all night long. He has a sleep disorder; he needs the fan's sound to block out all the little sounds that wake him up. We both watch the NBA championships. This is what I hear: Each time Shaquille scores a basket, he, my neighbour, makes an ecstatic, painful sound as if he is entering Shaquille's body, inhabiting Shaquille's powerful arms, his beautiful head, leaping into Shaquille as Shaquille leaps in the air. The sound my neighbour makes startles me. It is guttural yet it soars; it is sexual, it hits every register of passion. I stop watching the game; halt my own dance into Damon Stoudamire's bouncy legs, his speed and fakes. This is entering the body valued.

Or when while watching the Olympics in Seoul, the whole nation, Canada, entered the body of Ben Johnson for 9.79 seconds; entered his thick muscular legs tuned to their powerful swiftness, his determined face, his breathing precisioned and loose, the entire locomotion of him straining to contain our invasions and break the tape. The utter victory of him, the fabulous elation, when the nation and he reached beyond what it was humanly possible to do, which is the quest of humanity. And then several hours later the unceremonious decamping when his steroid use was discovered, the nation fleeing from his body like parasites fleeing a skeleton which had now become the evil Black body. The body valued and cursed in 9.79 seconds.

I am not suggesting that only whites enter Black bodies. I am suggesting that we all enter the Black body embracing its symbolisms. Inhabiting the Black body is also an act in which Blacks engage. We all take part in its mask, its performance. The Black body is a common possession, a consumer item. Technology has made this possible even beyond the borders of the original discourse. So that a young person in Azerbaijan or Texas or Istanbul or Stockholm can embody Michael Jordan with an innocence which belies but nevertheless witnesses the loaded narrative.

Looking at Black Entertainment Television's *Midnight Love*, a music video show, I notice the extreme sexualizing of both the male and the female Black body. It is not the colonizing watcher who creates these bodies; these extremely sexualized bodies are created, and inhabited or invaded, by Black women and men themselves. It is a curiously complicated doubleness. The Black person inhabits the Black body which is a cipher of the dreams, memories, horrors, and fears of Black bodies, in a performance of sexuality cut through with racialized assumptions of the Black body as "overly" sexual (whatever Puritanism that concept contains). This performance is primarily for an audience of Black people who are invited to join in this inhabiting and invading. The performances themselves are further exaggerations of sexual prowess; the sexual prowess is itself performance. At times inadvertent and at times mocking, these videos execute the racialized fantasy of the Black body.

The trope of captivity is so compelling that it is curiously entwined in interpretations of romantic love. In a playful song, "911," full of double entendre, singers Wyclef and Mary J. Blige sing to each other that someone should call the police for their heartbreak. They infer that this love of theirs would get them life in prison. Or when rappers Ja Rule and Vita rap

"Put It on Me" they enact a scene with Ja Rule in prison having left his lover set up outside with an expensive house and jewellery. They rap of a love that will survive incarceration. In one line Ja Rule tellingly signifies that the world does not belong to Black people else he would give it to his lover.

## 4

How to describe this mix of utter, hopeless pain and elation leaning against this door? Caribana, on Lakeshore Boulevard in the city of Toronto. There are some one million people there, some are costumed, all are in the throes of the most unfettered pleasure; dancing, singing, joking, eating. This is the major Black festival in Canada, Caribbean in origin, Black now in enactment. For there are Blacks from the United States who make the trek to Toronto for the festival. Among the million there are myriad "origins." Flags representing these origins are wrapped around heads, torsos, and legs, carried in hats, in hands, and by babies. Every once in a while a band leader or DJ comes along and calls out these origins: "Anybody from . . . ?" placing a country or territory after the preposition, to which there are screamed acknowledgements from sections of the crowd. The carnival itself is situated in slavery. It was a celebration of Black liberation from forced labour during that period when people would mock the dress and parody the ways of slave owners, when they would claim their souls as free from the slavery of their bodies in shows of artistry and imagination. Here, dancing along the lakeshore, there is ecstasy, abandon, the graceful intelligence of the body. Well, perhaps it's not such a paradox after all. Though the meanings are always slipping. This dreary door which I've been thinking about, though its effects are unremitting, does not claim the human being unremittingly. All that emanates from it is not dread but also creativity. This comes to me as I am standing, listening to the music, mouthing an inane soca lyric that commands me to jump or shake.

*"Pray for a life without plot, a day without narrative."*

1

I happened on this line by Derek Walcott in his book *The Bounty*. I cannot know precisely what he means but I recognized something in it. Or perhaps something in it called me. It described perfectly my desire for relief from the persistent trope of colonialism. To be without this story of captivity, to dis-remember it, or to have this story forget me, would be heavenly. But of course in that line too is the indifference, the supplication of prayer. Yet I want to think that perhaps there is also regeneration in its meaning.

"We need to have a cognitive schema as well as practic
mastery of way-finding . . ." To reclaim the Black body from
that domesticated, captive, open space is the creative project
always underway. There are many stories, fables, and secrets
in the Diaspora about the way home to Africa. In Toni
Morrison's novel *Song of Solomon*, Milkman Dead's great-
grandfather flies off to Africa; a song remains in the folk-
lore, "a song" which leads Milkman to his own flight of
salvation in the arms of his friend Guitar.

> *O Solomon don't leave me here*
> *Cotton balls to choke me*
> *O Solomon don't leave me here?*
> *Bukra's arms to yoke me*
> *Solomon done fly, Solomon done gone*
> *Solomon cut across the sky, Solomon gone home.*

Stories of Africans flying home to Africa or walking home
on the ocean floor abound in continental America and the
archipelago. Africans born in Africa were said to know how
to fly. If when they arrived in the Americas, one legend has
it, they did not eat salt, they could fly back home. Salt
would weigh them down or turn their blood.

There is a story of a woman, enslaved, called Gang Gang
Sarah who walked up the hill at Moriah, Tobago, climbed

the silk cotton tree, and flew all the way back to Africa.

When I was a child, old people told these stories with the greatest equanimity, perhaps only lowering their voices as if telling an important secret in case one needed, at another time, a way out.

In Julie Dash's film *Daughters of the Dust*, upon reaching the shores of the Americas the captured turn and walk back into the water, their chains weighing them down, their faith of return unflagging.

A relative of mine was said to have walked out into the water at Guaya. Flinging his ring back to shore, he instructed it, "Go tell them I'm drowning." I do not know if he was trying to find his way home.

One may not call these ways practical but they certainly suggest a mastery of way-finding. So much so that no known map is necessary, nor any known methods of conveyance. Except escaping the body.

The religious ritual across North and South America and the archipelago of being inhabited by the gods, goddesses, and spirits of Africa may be another method of way-finding. A neighbour from my childhood once told me that she was a

Shango mother and that she knew many people who could go back to Africa when they "caught the power." Another even further back in my memory, one called Neighbour Lorna, lived in a house whose yard she had turned into a shrine, when at night the scent of a certain white flower emanated. She was said to deal in spirits whose renown came straight from Africa. She could inveigle them to help the lonely, the heartbroken, the sick, or the wicked.

Getting to the Door of No Return then needs no physical apparatus except the mind; the body is the prison. It is the body which makes the sign for sanction and regulation. It precedes its appearances, forecasting . . . It is why Baby Suggs performs the spiritual ritual of reclaiming and cleansing the body in the clearing in Toni Morrison's *Beloved*.

> *"Here," she said, "in this place, we flesh; flesh that weeps, laughs; flesh that dances on bare feet in grass. Love it. Love it hard. Yonder they do not love your flesh. They despise it. They do not love your eyes; they'd just as soon pick 'em out. No more do they love the skin on your back. Yonder they flay it. And o my people they do not love your hands. Those they only use, tie, bind, chop off and leave empty. Love your hands! Love them."*

## 2

The North Star, the Big Dipper, a dark sky, a clear night, a rabbit's foot, a juju bag, maljo beads, holy water, water of compassion, success powder, single bible leaf. Signs of rescue. With these their only compasses Africans escaped slavery in the Americas, made their way to remote places, maroonages. These signs were not signs to the way home but signs to somewhere free of signs for the body. But of course by this time the Black body was so freighted with the excesses and needs of the New World culture that even somewhere free was not quite sufficient. The signs did not fall away.

## 3

*Guardian Weekly*, March 30–April 5, 2000
(Austria)

*. . . In January this year, when police raided the home of Black Africans in Trainskuche. "One hundred and forty police stormed the home looking for drugs, but nothing was found," he [a witness] said. "They then carried out painful anal searches, simply because there was some suspicion that there might be drugs there. All you need is a black face to be considered suspicious." . . . The focal point of Amnesty's allegations is the case of 25-year-old Marcus Omofuma, a Nigerian asylum seeker, who died while being deported from Vienna to Sofia in May last*

*year. He was bound and gagged "like a mummy stuck to the seat" by the three officers who accompanied him, and arrived unconscious in Sofia where doctors pronounced him dead. No charges were brought.*

"New York Times," Jack E. White
(*Time*, June 7, 1999)

*Suppose that on one fateful night in August 1997, New York City cop Justin Volpe had contented himself with pummeling Abner Louima with his nightstick instead of ramming a broom handle into Louima's rectum and then waving it in front of his face. Suppose that after that vicious assault, Volpe had not pranced around the precinct house with the blood-and-feces-stained stick, inviting other cops to examine it. . . . There would be a good chance that we would never have heard of Louima and that Volpe would still be patrolling the beat in Brooklyn.*

(*Time*, October 19, 2000)

*Diallo, an unarmed African immigrant living in the Bronx, was shot 41 times by four white police officers. . . . A police detective testified that Diallo's body was so riddled with bullets that some actually fell out of him as he was taken away from the scene.*

## 4

There are other bodies in the world which are brutalized. These examples are not a case for exclusivity. Women in Afghanistan are entombed alive in burquas. The Taliban has forced them out of the public space; one cannot help but think that these men wish all women dead. They seem to require more than subservience, as they've constructed a vanishing of hundreds of thousands of women. There are countless other examples of brutalized bodies, bodies which play a role as talisman and sign. Not sobered by the emaciated bodies of death camps of the Holocaust, Europe revived these spectres in Bosnia. An endless parade of starved and famined bodies of ghostlike children in Ethiopia, Sudan, and Eritrea find television cameras and rich countries unaffected and racially superior. So, no, these examples are not a case for exclusivity, only for a certain particularity. A particularity which has its resonances against those other brutalized bodies.

## 5

The thing is that I think Blacks in the Diaspora carry the Door of No Return in our senses. It is a passport which, after boarding the plane, we are unable to make disappear by tearing it up and throwing it into the toilet. We arrive with its coat of arms, its love knot, its streamers, its bugle, its emblem attesting to our impossible origins. This passport is from the territory of the Door. The territory is vast, its nature shiftable. We are always in the middle of the journey.

I know many nationalists along this journey. Each square foot of the Americas has its nationalism. And probably the most powerful of these nationalisms can be experienced in the U.S. But Jamaica, Brazil, Antigua, even the volcanic Montserrat are no less virulent. There are flags and anthems, even a real love for each place — the ways and objects and events which collect into nations. But the Door of No Return opens all nationalisms to their imaginative void.

One stands on a street corner in Ocho Rios or in a market-place in Montevideo or at a newspaper kiosk in Chicago or Sofia, one stands there and imagines another territory, another history, and in that moment the fake emblems fall away. The cigarette falls from the fingers, its light singing into the gutter, the newspaper rustles in a catch of alien wind, the passion fruit feels leaden in the hand at the market, and one simply cannot make sense of one's time or one's unas-suageable desire; one feels a strange discomfort and one sighs and takes off again into a life, a life against oneself.

6

To live at the Door of No Return is to live self-consciously. To be always aware of your presence as a presence outside of yourself. And to have "others" constantly remark on your presence as outside of itself. If to think is to exist, then we exist doubly. An ordinary conversation is never an ordinary conversation. One cannot say the simplest thing without doubling or being doubled for the image that emerged from the doorway. At a party you remark enthusiastically that you have been away, someplace where the sun has deliciously deepened the shade of your skin, and you look up from your bronzed shoulder to bewilderment. The self which is unobservable is a mystery. The mystery also plays out in the "private" space of the family in the Diaspora, where light or dark shading is related as proximity to the Door of No Return and to its secret ineffable quality. This mystery evades all the simplest powers of discernment in the public space. Every space you occupy is public space, that is, space which is definable by everyone. That is, the image which emerges from the Door of No Return is public property belonging to a public exclusive of the Black bodies which signify it. One is aware of this ownership. One is constantly refuting it, or ignoring it, or troubling it, or parodying it, or tragically reaffirming it.

7

Blacks in the Diaspora obscure themselves as much as they are obscured. They observe and rectify incessantly. Hair, skin tone, talk, fashion. Fashions are not fashions at all but refashioning; language is not communication but reinvention. They are never in place but on display. Curiously the dynamism of these circumlocutions are the wellspring of culture in the Americas and with the dubious help of mass marketing they are the creative legs of an even more dubious globalization. Let me break it down. What is called Black culture, including aesthetic tastes and sensibilities, is used daily as creative backdrop to multinational markets. But more interestingly, what is produced in Black homes, and neighbourhoods, the simplest exchanges in communities — expressions, gestures, understandings, dress — these are taken up in the generalizing, homogenizing culture. In the language, for example; certain colloquialisms created in a city block of New York or Oakland or Kingston, Jamaica or Ladbrooke Grove, London become communal sayings far beyond.

8

This self which is unobservable is a mystery. It is imprisoned in the observed. It is constantly struggling to wrest itself from the warp of its public ownerships. Its own language is plain yet secret. Rather, obscured.

9

If I can say it. Let me. I think that Blacks in the Diaspora feel captive despite the patent freedom we experience, despite the fact that we are several hundred years away from the Door of No Return, despite the fact that the door does not exist; despite the fact that we live in every state of self-agency, some exceedingly powerful, some less so of course but self-agency nonetheless. One might even argue for the sheer magnificence of our survival against history. Yet . . .

## Maps

A portolan — a written description of the course along which ships sailed, indicating bays, capes, coves, ports, magnetic rhumb lines, and the distances between places.

## Finding a Compass

### 1

It is 4:45 a.m. I awake in the foreign country of silence. The lone intermittent car going by; someone trying to find shelter or someone running from it. I am doing what I do every time I drink too much wine and wake up suddenly at 4:45 a.m. I read. Eduardo Galeano falls open at this time: "I'm nostalgic for a country which doesn't yet exist on a map."

## 2

In cities at 4:45 a.m., Toronto or Calgary or Halifax, there are
these other inhabitants of silence. Two hundred miles outside,
north of any place, or in the middle of it, circumnavigating
absence. For a moment it is a sweet country, in that moment
you know perhaps someone else is awake reading Galeano.

## 3

At seventeen on Raglan Avenue, it wasn't wine but loneli-
ness that woke me up to reach for Prevert, whose *Paroles* I
had found in an old book shop. "Pierre tell me the truth"
hissing through my sleep. Unable to leave those two in that
street, *Rue de Seine*, in the middle of hopelessness. The man
with the hat and the raincoat, the woman who "has a furi-
ous desire to live." Both of them in the middle of war and
therefore impossible questions. Perhaps at seventeen I too
felt in the middle of war with forces arrayed against the
pleasure of being human. The German occupation of
France was Prevert's canvas. The ubiquitous occupation of
coloniality, mine. I didn't put this into those words then. I
only felt an affinity across a continent, thirty years, and a
translation of his words into English.

## 4

The street on the north side of St. Clair between Bathurst
and Vaughan was a small one lodging a mix of people:

Europeans, Africans, Indians. The superintendent of the building I lived in drank heavily. His face and that of his wife like paste softened in alcohol in the mornings. My neighbour to the left was a man, a young Italian, who woke every morning at five to go to his job in construction. On Saturday nights he bombarded my left wall with music that sounded like crashing machinery. The woman across the hall was saving every penny of her money to send to St. Vincent and the Grenadines for her mother. Someone downstairs decided to take up the recorder, and to my right was a neighbour who complained to the super about my three-month-old nephew crying all night with colic.

The view from this apartment was wonderful. Another building filled with windows into other apartments. A middle-aged eastern European woman in flowered dresses; how could I tell she was eastern European. I couldn't. I assumed by the light frills around her shoulders. The knick-knacks on the windowsill. The not-quite-here feel of her. She could have been from anywhere, really. A man, probably English, with a small hawk's face, who drank coffee incessantly and looked worriedly out the window. I'd say he had no work; I'd say he was in his forties. He smoked cigarettes to the quick. A window with a dark red curtain which didn't open. Two students, male, the apartment curtainless and scruffy, beer bottles on the windowsill. A cat at another window whose job it was to watch me watching. A few other lights are on at 4:45 a.m., the people there thinking of their own rough doorways. I never saw a party through those windows. Why, I wonder. I loved looking at the slow, unimportant movement of those lives — the flowerpots and beer bottles, the evening incandescence of the window frames.

<br>

## 5

One time in Antigonish, Nova Scotia, when it was winter and when my head was thick with questions, John Arthur Murphy met me off the bus from Halifax and took me to his house, where his wife gave me a warm quilt. John Arthur made jokes, his body stiffened and pained with arthritis, his children wanting to be lifted up anyway, and we talked about another war. Another country where we had stood in a room together with people dancing and talking about revolution. Then the next day, all of us, the internationalists, had boarded a bus and driven out to see farms as if we knew anything about them at all. The poor farmers impressed us with heads of lettuce growing but more with how weak our own bodies were and how childish our plans and our visit. John Arthur joked self-effacingly. After the war there, John Arthur Murphy met me half-dead and dazed at that bus in Antigonish. I remember that quilt and John Arthur's body, which fought its own conflict.

6

Every identity is irremediably destabilized by its
"exterior."

Chantal Mouffe

7

Water is another country. We are in Charlottesville boarding a small boat to head out to sea. The two men running
the boat look at us, sizing us up to see if we are fit for the
journey. One of them says, "It might get rainy." We ask,
"Well, should we still go?" The other says, "Oh, yes, no
problem. The water is as smooth as a baby's bottom."
Assured and amused, we climb on. The two men head for
the shade of the canopy on the dory. We sit out in the sun.
Leleti sits on the prow. I grip one of the seating planks;
Margaret grips another. We are bare headed. We are heading out to nowhere in particular. The sea is another country. The two men know the landmarks. Swells succeed us
and precede us like mountains rising and subsiding. The
crinkle of the water changes shade every millisecond. The
ocean feels like land. The two men point out this or that
area as if it were a patch of ground, a small hill, or an inhabited vista. Fishing boats whiz by us over the next watery hill,
thin fishing rods antennaed to the side give them the look
of insects flitting.

# 8

I see two men through a keyhole; one is my grandfather, the other is the man who is supposed to be my father. My grandfather is saying something quietly. The man who is supposed to be my father is a man dressed as if he is from another country. My grandfather is commanding him softly. The man who is supposed to be my father has given me a butternut candy; it is wrapped in gold and brown cellophane paper. My grandfather is moving him, the man who is supposed to be my father, off the doorstep with his quiet language. I am sucking the sweet nutty juice of the candy as my grandfather speaks gently, perhaps threateningly. The man who is supposed to be my father, his mother is from another country. She puts on airs. She thinks her son too good for us. Her son is a scamp. He hangs behind his mother's dress-tail. He has no scruples. He has no pride. My grandfather cautions him with incorruptible civility. The man who is supposed to be my father moves outside of the frame of the keyhole. My grandfather's white shirt cuff raises itself and disappears; he steps toward the man who is supposed to be my father, who is himself out of sight. I see my grandfather's moustache as he turns toward the unseen man who is supposed to be my father whose mother is "Portugee" and from another country. My grandfather is unimpressed by the fading unscrupulous man who is drifting into the street beyond the hibiscus fence. The quiet of

my grandfather, as he tells the man never to step in our
doorway, is as ironed as my grandfather's white shirt, as
pressed as the disciplined seam in his trousers, as blistering
as the shine on his black shoes.

## 9

In the room at 4:45 a.m. Aimé Césaire is writing:

> *I should discover once again the secret of great*
> *communication and great combustions. I*
> *should say storm. I should say river. I should*
> *say tornado. I should say leaf. I should say tree.*
> *I should be wet by all rains, made damp with*
> *all dews.*

In the room at 4:50 a.m., reading this, I decide to be a poet.
Césaire is still writing:

> *And you ghosts rise bluely from the chemistry*
> *of a forest of hunted beasts, twisted machines*
> *jujube trees of rotted flesh, a basket of oysters*
> *of eyes, a lace of straps cut in the beautiful sisal of the skin.*
> *I have words vast enough to*
> *contain you and you, earth, tense drunken earth, . . .*

10

At 4:45 a.m. the Door of No Return is visible. Bowed to a page, the pen moves in scars. One's body emerging naked through its rough portal. One can feel the stone of its sides with one's hands, and that is how I felt at 4:45 a.m.

## Maps

In an early essay in *The Overcrowded Barracoon*, V.S. Naipaul wrote, "Yet always the obvious is overwhelming. One is a traveller and as soon as the dread of a particular district has been lessened by familiarity, it is time to move on again, through vast tracts which will never become familiar, which will sadden and the urge to escape will return." Written in 1962 for the *Illustrated Weekly of India*, it is an essay about travelling in India called "In the Middle of the Journey." These two sentences occur among many mis-sightings of India and Indians that Naipaul describes in his book. He is determined, it seems at the outset, to conclude that India is wanting in some sociopathic way — the landscape is "monotonous," its "simplicity" is "frightening," its people are Philistine and myopic. The essay mentions wanting to escape or wanting to separate himself from the country. The essay is less interesting for what it may offer by way of any description of India than for Naipaul's choices of words and emotions that indicate his state of mind. Of course India is overwhelming, of course it is vast, but that does not give one the sense of dread that Naipaul attaches to these words. This dread one suspects arrived with him. The stories he must have heard as a child of the Kala Pani, the black water of the journey of indentured labourers from India to the Caribbean, the experience of those workers for whom India might have been both a curse from which they left or a haven from which they were plucked. When Naipaul travels to India to send this report he is making the return trip across the Kala Pani . . . the Sargasso . . . the middle passage . . . the door: "Vast tracts which will never become familiar, which will sadden." They will never become familiar because two generations have missed their shape, more than one hundred years have passed since his family has been there. It exists only in memory, which is sometimes untrustworthy; it exists in the stories of his family passed down, each image dependent on the storyteller's gifts and skills.

Many read Naipaul as spiteful; even his former best friend Paul Theroux has confirmed that spitefulness (though we might question how a man can stay friends with another for half a lifetime and remain as pure as Theroux). But in some ways I read Naipaul as spitefully sorrowful. Like Morrison's character Beloved. Those vast tracts which will never become familiar are not merely description of a physical landscape but discourse on ancestral estrangement and filial longing. The dread he feels in the essay and the urge to escape are even more interesting. It is the dread of the unknown, the unfamiliar, the possibility of rejection — the same possibilities which faced Henry Louis Gates on his televisual journey back to Africa — the possibility that in fact one is unwanted back home, perhaps hated, perhaps even forgotten. The wound of forced exile generations ago is made more acute by indifference, by forgetfulness. No one in India remembers him or the experience he represents. Yet he carries within him this particularly accursed ancestral memory and this crushing dislocation of the self which the landscape does not solve. Instead he finds himself afraid and wishing to escape — to escape the "endless repetition of exhaustion and decay." To anyone else this sounds like merely "life" — its existential dilemma. To the descendants of the nineteenth-century Indian and African Diaspora, a nervous temporariness is our existential dilemma, our descent quicker, our decay faster, our existence far more tenuous; the routine of life is continually upheaved by colonial troublings. We have no ancestry except the black water and the Door of No Return. They signify space and not land. A "vastness" indeed "beyond imagination." It is not India which is beyond imagination; it is the black water.

Fear is repeated so many times in his essay, Naipaul in fact admits that "the despair lies more with the observer than the people." Though his admission is an attempt to be superior, his language here and all through the essay betrays someone trying to get a grasp of himself; trying to grasp something unfathomable, not in a landscape or in the regularity of abject poverty or slovenly wealth, but in oneself, in one's connection to anything. The superior voice of the text is directed to a particular audience in the metropole in which he has a provisional footing; the fear leaks out as an expression of that self-doubting, self-conscious being who is at the core of the discourse — author and autobiographer. Naipaul's subsequent books on India grow more self-assured in the former project, his voice more veiled and recalcitrant. But always spotted in between for those who wish to read there is that personal wounding, still fresh — fresher still the older it grows.

## 1

Origins. A city is not a place of origins. It is a place of transmigrations and transmogrifications. Cities collect people, stray and lost and deliberate arrivants. Origins are rehabilitated and rebuilt here. A torturer in Chile becomes a taxi driver, an English thief becomes a stock hawker, an Eritrean warlord becomes a bicycle courier. An Indian businessman a security guard, a Hong Kong policeman a waiter, a sixth-generation Ukrainian girl a murderer, a teacher from the Caribbean a housekeeper, a farmer from Azores a construction worker.

A city is a place where the old migrants transmogrify into citizens with disappeared origins who look at new migrants as if at strangers, forgetting their own flights. And the new migrants remain immigrants until they too can disappear their origins.

## 2

Belonging. A friend of mine told me this story. It was emancipation day 1998 in Kingston, Jamaica. The prime minister of Ghana was on a state visit. He was making a speech to a great gathering for these celebrations when a delegation of Rastafarians requesting to speak to him pressed toward the stage. He continued speaking about the wonderful developments in Jamaica, the long way they had come from slavery, etc. The Rastafarians continued their urgings to have a word with him. Security tried to keep them back, but they pressed on toward the stage. Finally the prime minister addressed them again, declaiming his admiration for the country. They, cutting him off, said to him in exasperation, "But we want to go home!" Home meaning Africa.

## 3

Home. I was never sure that I wanted to go home. I liked the streets of the city. I liked other people's houses, other people's lives. I would look into a yard and imagine there a life unlike mine. I did not imagine this because mine was unhappy; I only imagined it because it was possible to imagine. Home suggests order and routine, tradition, family. Someone else's order struck me as fascinating — truthfully, suffocating. I would pass by those same houses at night and feel a sense of suffocation, enclosure, cloister. Houses with a single light, perhaps a bit of the radio playing, a child's voice; these houses, so secure, seemed stifling. It was as if they said that there was no more about the world to happen, no more to know.

## 4

Too much has been made of origins. All origins are arbitrary. This is not to say that they are not also nurturing, but they are essentially coercive and indifferent. Country, nation, these concepts are of course deeply indebted to origins, family, tradition, home. Nation-states are configurations of origins as exclusionary power structures which have legitimacy based solely on conquest and acquisition. Here at home, in Canada, we are all implicated in this sense of origins. It is a manufac- tured origin nevertheless playing to our need for home, however tyrannical. This country, in the main a country of immigrants, is always redefining origins, jockeying and smarming for degrees of belonging. Erasing aspects of compli- cated origins by shedding accents, shedding dress, shedding tastes, shedding tyrannies; taking on other aspects of other complicated origins no matter the new tyrannies. Entry into nation and therefore home pervades the public discourse.

## 5

In 1999 a ship carrying children, teenagers, from China was apprehended off the coast of British Columbia. Newspapers and televisions referred to them as "migrants" and migrants they no doubt were, but one cannot help reading the exclusion of these "migrants" from the category of "children," which would make it possible to include them in a definition of family reserved for the people within the nation. All the accoutrement of outsider could then be brought to regulate and choreograph their appearance both on the television screens and in newspaper photographs as well as the interior of the body politic.

## 6

This irony in the *New York Times*, Friday, December 11, 1998:

> *American and Canadian authorities announced today that they had broken up a sophisticated ring that smuggled Chinese immigrants into the United States and ultimately to New York City, through a Mohawk reservation along the border. The authorities said the ring made up primarily of Chinese citizens and members of the Mohawk tribe, transported more than 3600 Chinese immigrants*

*across the lightly patrolled border along the St Lawrence*
*River and into upstate New York during the last two years.*
*"This is the first large-scale alien smuggling operation we*
*have encountered on the northern border," Doris Meissner,*
*the Commissioner of the Immigration and Naturalisation*
*Service, said in announcing the indictments.*

One wants to ask who better able or authorized to give safe
passage to anyone across North America than the Mohawk
or any of the people who inhabited this continent before its
New World settlers. Nevertheless, the language of the piece
asserts the identities "American" and "Canadian" as dominant over "Mohawk" and "Chinese."

The piece continues:

*Today's announcement highlighted the extent to which the*
*28-square-mile Indian reservation that straddles two*
*Canadian provinces and one American state has become a*
*haven for smugglers. The foggy creeks and wooded islands*
*of the Indian territory which is known as the St Regis*
*Mohawk reservation on the American side and the*
*Akwesasne Indian territory in Canada, have long been*
*used to spirit gasoline, cigarettes, tobacco and drugs between*
*the two countries. In recent years more and more of the*
*contraband has been human. . . . A look at a map shows*

*you how easy it is to use the place as a vehicle for smuggling.*
*It isn't just aliens, though . . .*

Notice how this territory is wrapped in the crypto-fascist romances of both dominant nations — the "foggy creeks," the "wooded islands," and foundational to this romance, the "human contraband." Hundreds of years after the making of its neo-origins these Canadians and Americans who police these fresh borders, materially as well as intellectually, play and dwell in the same language of their conquest. A language which summons mystery and wilderness. The passage could have been written two hundred years ago.

### 7

Some of us want entry into the home and nation that are signified by these romances. Some of us in the Diaspora long so for nation — some continuous thread of biological or communal association, some bloodline or legacy which will cement our rights in the place we live. The problem of course is that even if those existed — and they certainly do, even if it is in the human contraband which we represent in the romance — they do not guarantee nation for Blacks in the Diaspora.

A piece in *The Globe and Mail,* Friday, November 28, 1998, gives us a sense of this: *"Thousands of Black slaves fought for the British in the American Revolution on the promise they would get their freedom and land after the war. But after the British lost and thousands of loyalists fled to Nova Scotia from New England states, the 3,500 Blacks among them had two fears: that they would be sent back to their masters under the mutual Slave Act and that they would starve waiting to get land.*" Starve they did, or were driven out of towns to barren and desolate reaches. Some left to resettle in Sierra Leone. The British Loyalists transmuted into the Canadian nation, the Black Loyalists found themselves immutable.

It is of course tempting to try to enter this nation of Canada. It is even more tempting to see that desire as a rightful thing. Fugitives from slavery, Black Loyalists, sleeping car porters, immigrant workers — from the earliest Black presence to the present it would be easy, given the terms of entry for white settlers and immigrants, to presume that these same terms can be legitimately used to cement such a right. The right to nation. What we have to ask ourselves is, as everyone else in the nation should ask themselves also, nation predicated on what?

## 8

I am driving toward Eglinton Avenue, about to leave the city. Going toward the Allen Expressway I take Oakwood, stop at the Petro-Canada to fill up before taking the highway. It is winter. I always fill up here on my way up north. The same man, in his thirties, dark hair, Italian, comes out of the office. I pop the gas lid, lower the window. It is redundantly cold. Old snow is piled up anywhere there's space. It is rusty and muddy and oily; it is so old some of it is stone. The man is wearing a red down vest; he pats his body, removes one glove to lift the gas nozzle. I ask him, not wanting to know but just to be courteous, "How're you doing . . . cold, eh?" He shapes his face to emit a sigh of resignation and says, "This is not a country to live in. It's a country to make money, but not a country to live." Can I tell him otherwise? We both shrug in acknowledgement of the deep truth he's just articulated. And the lie just beside it. I pay him and head for the highway.

## 9

Too much has been made of origins. And so if I reject this notion of origins I have also to reject its mirror, which is the sense of origins used by the powerless to contest power in a society. The overstrong arguments about "culture," which are made both by defenders of what is "Canadian" as well as defenders of what is labelled "immigrant." These are mirror/image–image/mirror of each other and are invariably conservative. Because they must draw very definite borders both to contain their constituencies as well as, in the case of the powerful, to aggressively exclude the other and, in the case of the powerless, to weakly do the same while waving a white flag to the powerful for inclusion. Each of these arguments select and calcify origins. Out of a multiplicity of stories, they cobble together a narrative glossing over accident, opportunism, necessity, and misdirection. They uplift aggression and carnage into courage, they exaggerate cunning into pride. In opposition to the calcified Canadian nation narrative we read calcified hyphenated narratives, without exception, from all other groups in the nation which stand outside of that narrative.

## 10

A brief look at a Black community newspaper in Toronto reveals a swagger of superlative claims — "Canada's largest ethnic paper" and "making our voice heard"; an epidemic of crossnationalist beauty pageants — Miss Guyana Canada, Miss Africa Canada, for which twelve beauties would vie; a film festival called the "other film festival"; news stories intoning this same crossnationalism and "otherness" about West Indian family days in Etobicoke; Grenadian Canadians honouring a doctor; making desserts *à la* Jamaica; a mother who is refused a visa to see her daughter who died unexpectedly in Canada; an editorial about the differential treatment of Black festivals by city officials and police in the city; numerous articles on religion and faith. Surrounding these stories is a veritable blizzard of advertisements for travel deals to every Caribbean location and New York, Detroit, and Buffalo, bolstered by ads for shipping barrels to every Caribbean location, buttressed by an intimidating phalanx of ads for immigration lawyers, overlaid with ads for goat, coconut milk, and red snapper, and finally riotously decked out with ads for banquet halls, reggae celebrations, and calypso extravangazas.

How do we read these complicated juxtapositions of belonging and not belonging, belonging and intrabelonging. In a place such as this, so full of immigrants, everyone is deeply interested in belonging. The Blacks addressed in this newspaper are in the main of Caribbean origin, which is not to say the half of it. They switch from the more specific nationalisms of island and territory to region throughout their discourse with Canada. They also gesture to the continent of Africa and at times also to India and China, since there are several diasporas that come together in those Caribbean origins. They claim a Canada qualified by these tenuous origins. They quarrel with the Canadian nation on counts of racism and exclusion from kind treatment. They travel — journey — back and forth from these origins to their neo-origins. They are legally embattled with the Canadian nation-state on points of physical entry into the nation. Their pleasures and desires seem human enough: food and music.

11

The imperative for these crossnationalisms bores me. It puts into play an exhausting, stultifying set of practices which are repeated and repeated without change. It makes people cling to the most narrow of definitions of culture and identity, and deploy the most banal characteristics as exemplary. National identity is a dance of artificiality, since what it dances must essentially be unchanging. Some would say, well, no, Canadian identity has changed over the last thirty or fifty years. Not at all. We are drawn constantly to the European shape in its definition. A shape, by the way, which obscures its own multiplicity. And when we read the hyphenated narratives we see the angst produced by this unchanging quality.

12

Why consider the Door of No Return? Because it exists without prompting. It exists despite all efforts to obscure it or change it or reinterpret it by its carpenters or its passengers. The Door of No Return is ocular. It is propitious. From it one may reflect, grasp.

13

*Roads*

I dreamed of Gabriel García Márquez. He needed a pen and I searched for one, giving him one, then another, then finally a fountain pen with peacock blue ink.

Once I dreamed of Wilson Harris and a steep slate incline of mountain with a river below and the sound of strange birds. Once I had Neruda within sight, on a bus on a cold night in China, a cold night of old faces, a night of intentions.

### Compass

That dislocation, that suddenly not knowing where you are or from which point to ascertain your bearings. A point of certainty, a "where" from which to sort out the next destination.

I recall as a child spending hours in the ocean, or what seemed like hours to a child at any rate. I would spend hours there in the water, emerging legs heavy and disoriented. On those days when I simply could not leave the ocean, running back time and again to fall into it when I was called out, I would later dream of being floated and rocked. I would dream of the ocean at my throat rocking and swelling. I liked these dreams. Lying in my sleep I would feel as if I were still in the sea, my head dipped in the water, the sharp disconcerting taste of water in my nostrils, the feeling of breathing water instead of air.

The first thing I saw, imagined, was water, an ocean full of turquoise water. We lived in a small wooden house on the small shore of the Atlantic at Guayguayare. Standing on the beach at Guaya against the broad ocean I thought of cities, faraway places I had read of. Before I could read I only thought of the water, the fish and the fishermen I had seen come and go in it, the bits of wood, the shells, the ships which only browed the horizon, the frothy ripples which spread to my feet, the river foaming to its mouth up the beach, the new gifts of green and blue bottles and objects worn by the sea beyond recognition. The ocean there always gave me a sense of leavings and arrivals. Of momentous happenings, a fish caught, a dead body washed up, a sign from god — a too red sky, a too blue sky, frigate birds coming in, an empty boat washed in, fishermen lost or run away, muddy weedy water, blood in the sea.

The centre of the world was the beach at Guaya. From there radiated the world. Venezuela was to the southeast, Brazil to the southwest, Britain to the northeast, America to the northwest. A road map, compressed to fit the six-inch scroll of a grape leaf; these were my possible directions and my desires. This road map worked as it had for the Romans recording distance and not topography; since only the ocean lay in between, it recorded plans and not speculation. In other words, it was to be my itinerary.

I had planned to marry a fisherman and move to Venezuela. I had planned to be misled and mishandled by a bad man and run off to Brazil with him. I had planned to live in London. I had planned to live in New York City.

*June 1999, London, England*

In 1897 the British sacked the city of Benin, carrying off the great works of art — sculptures in brass, terra cotta, bronze, and ivory. I've been here several times. I know this place. How? It is not any country I've lived in, yet it is a country I have lived in. I do not know these particular people with whom I'm walking on the street, yet I know them. I do not know that if I walk this street in this direction I will end up at a roundabout, yet I know it. I know the narrowness of the street; I know the circus I'm walking toward. I know the pace of other pedestrians and I know how long I will have to wait at a coffee shop to be noticed and then to ask for my coffee. I know all this because it is England.

One week ago I arrived at the airport and all my apprehension on the plane about a foreign country — suspicious customs officers who flag my skin for scrutiny and my anxiousness at the prospect of finding my way to this city — all my apprehension subsided as I joined an oddly familiar queue of South Asians, Africans, Spanish, French, Arab, and Middle Eastern people struggling with papers, forgotten bags, crying children, lost purses, well-filed papers, swollen feet, and red-eyed sleeplessness. All nervousness subsided when I saw the same apprehension loosen in their faces as they saw me, too, like them part of an unnameable familiarity among us. Empire.

I know we marched into schools to the same classical music, we wore the same uniforms, we walked with writing slates hung around our necks, we sat at the same desks, we read from the same Royal Readers perhaps, we drank the same condensed milk, we ate the same butter from cows in Jersey or New Zealand, we tailored our speech in the presence of officialdom, we read the Brontës and Enid Blyton, we memorized Wordsworth and Walter Scott, we improbably dramatized Shakespeare, we stood in lines waving flags at completely indifferent royals, we sang English airs, we played London Bridge, we danced the maypole.

And here we were in a line entering England, a place we were all too familiar with and a place all too familiar with us. The customs man was affable, not suspicious as are the ones in Canada, whose passport I held. The ones back home who take me aside after my holidays and examine my folded clothing, handle my chunks of real cocoa, even after I have tried to dress in the least amount of clothing to allay suspicion of possible bags of marijuana strapped to my belly. Here, the clerk surprisingly says, "How long will you be stayin', luv?" There's an anxious woman in a green gold-trimmed sari behind me, then a man from Ghana, then a family from Morocco or Egypt. The British really understand about trade, travel, exploration. Close to a thousand years of foraging and conquest are preterite in this clerk's use of the familiar. He even smiles a genuine kind of smile not the quick smirk of my compatriots. He at least tries to disarm me and not over-power me. That is the test of true power. That is why I know how to dance the maypole, and how to sing that song which begins, "Oranges and Lemons said the bells of St. Clements . . . ," and how I knew "The Rime of the Ancient Mariner" by heart at thirteen. Charm, for god's sake. Not fear of inva-sion like back home in Canada. Which, there, is fear of course of oneself.

Landing in London is landing in the familiar. The British must have built every place they settled in according to the same city plans as London. How else would I know that walking down each main street I would come to a roundabout, that streets would angle and twist into an inner square, that the width of streets would summon in me a particular stride, that Charing Cross Road would be right where it was? No matter what the landscape it seemed they imposed the same plan of narrow streets, cobbled alleys, squares, and circuses. Then they laid government buildings along in the same brown- and red-bricked way. Then they filled these buildings with quiet incom-petence, occasioning long queues and fuming patience until graft and bribery suffused all transactions. In the line at Heathrow we all know each other, then. We have the same road maps in our heads. We've walked the same streets of colony.

Nothing to pillage here, though. If you wanted to sack this city you'd get stuck in the constant traffic gridlock. Though you stand at exhibits in museums envious. And thinking, what balls!


### May 2000, Sydney, Australia

The twenty hours to Sydney, Australia, were claustrophobic, though I read two books and slept stretched across three seats. Sleep is the thing. If you can get to sleep at all on a long flight the body isn't so rebellious when you land. I rarely sleep on planes. Economy is the new version of packin' 'em tight. Though this time you're paying for it. The flight to Honolulu, our midway stop, was half empty. I didn't speak to anyone. I hate talking to perfect strangers on a long flight. I hate talking to anyone on a plane. Give someone a look beyond twenty seconds and you will hear her whole life story. If you need stories, that is all right. But who can tell what the story will be or how interesting the storyteller. So I take no chances; I immediately take a book out or a pen and paper, indicating privacy. I can't remember anyone on that flight.

The city, Sydney, has the presumption of all New World cities — that it can erase history or reinterpret it. But it cannot help boasting about its victories. A statue of Queen

Victoria, pregnant with power, dominates a square. Old buildings which once housed prisoners no doubt are rehabilitated into museums. They hold sway over the city's architects, who cannot help but make all enclosures prison-like. Sunlight in this desert is blocked out on some streets by the heaviness of history. Someone tells me that Sydney is a very multicultural city. I can't see it. Multiculturalism is relative to the state of white fear. So is empathy. The prime minister cannot bring himself to apologize for past wrongs of genocide and massacre. I ask someone where the Aboriginal people are. They call out a neighbourhood to me. Redfern. In the newspaper there is a story about a reconciliation march across the harbour bridge, there is a debate about which and whether government ministers will attend.

A Maori friend, Briar, introduces me to an Aboriginal friend, Cathy. Cathy is a whirlwind of hipness and charm. And connections. She gets us tickets to see the sold-out play *Stolen*. It is a play about Aboriginal children taken away from their parents and communities and subjected to the terrors of abuse and displacement. Just like at home in Canada. The similarities don't end there. Before the play we three go to dinner. Uncannily, with the same sense of derision, cynicism, and hilarious absurdity, we talk about race in the countries in which we live. Briar says that ever since *Once Were Warriors* (a film from New Zealand), television and film producers want her to write the same characters. Representation becomes a stereotype. She is expected to always have a drunken fighting Maori man and a battered Maori woman in her scripts. Cathy says of the reconciliation march, reconciled to what, what have we got to reconcile? There's been no truth, what is this about reconciliation? We laugh. Strange to anyone else but us, we are laughing through this whole conversation. We are eating seafood at a little restaurant near the theatre. We laugh in recognition, we laugh like old friends, like people who live in the same country. Later we cry through the play and more when the actors step out of the play and tell the audience their own stolen stories.

August 2000. Three months later, I hear Redfern's been raided by police, sixteen people arrested for drugs, but everybody knows it's to clean up the city and intimidate Aboriginal people before the Sydney Olympics. Three months later, a Darwin court dismisses the suit of two Aboriginal people who were stolen and abused. Men came on horses and took the girl, who is now sixty-two, away; of the other, they say his mother's thumbprint was evidence that she gave him up willingly. The judge says that the sixty-year-long practice of forcibly taking children away from their families was a product of goodwill and that the government was not liable for the devastation of a generation of people.

*July 2000, Mannheim, Germany*

We have just come from Landau on the train. We decide to go outside the station at Mannheim to breathe some fresh air until our train to Mainz. For Leslie the trains are portentous. Her family was taken away in them fifty-eight years ago. These trains account for the life of her family after. More doors, no returns. It is a baffling place, the parts of Germany we are able to visit. I have grown up on films about the Second World War Germany, Nazism, the Holocaust. Germany is forever attached to these images. Not to mention the more recent treatment of Turkish and African immigrants nor the forever seething neo-Nazi presence of shaved-headed young people without a shred of humanity in them. Two days ago there were neo-Nazi marches in Berlin and Hamburg. Our hosts represent the opposite of all this. We are at a conference on identity at the University of Mainz. Mainz, where Gutenberg created movable type. We visit the Gutenberg museum, where there is a replica of his press. We visit the old manuscripts. In the cocoon of our conference we feel safe; when we venture outside into city streets and trains, in Frankfurt, Landau, Mainz, the feeling of safety falls away and we are plagued by the spectres of the war which hang here like eternal clouds. One imagines that our hosts are plagued by them, too. Only the brazen can say, "I was not here, I did not do this and feel that." One hears that all the time in Canada;

about what people feel they are and are not responsible for. People use these arguments as reasons for not doing what is right or just. It never occurs to them that they live on the cumulative hurt of others. They want to start the clock of social justice only when they arrived. But one is born into history, one isn't born into a void. And so Leslie stands at train stations in Germany cringing at the trains' punctuality.

On Tuesday we are at Koblenz-Landau University. A young Turkish man asks a question about writing: "When you start writing because it hurts so much, do you only write about racism?" I try to tell him, you don't write about racism, you write about life. It is life you must write about. It is life you must insist on. For him the distinction is inadequate and unhelpful. He asks again, but I cannot satisfy him.

We are running toward the train station in Landau. We are late. Just off the square there is a small street, a complicated statue, and then a house. One of our hosts says, "This is where Anne Frank's grandparents lived. You must see it." We are late for the train, have had lunch and drunk wine. We step into the strangest, most silent of courtyards. It is all wooden banisters and quiet. Light and silence pour into its centre.

*August 1984, Toronto, Canada*
A friend meets me on the street. He was born in the United States. He left there during the Vietnam War. He had refused to go to war, so he came to Canada rather than be put in jail. Agitated over American foreign policy everywhere, but mostly in Nicaragua, he says to me, "I'm cutting off diplomatic relations with them, man. I'm not even going to talk to my family. That's it. There's a whole bunch of Caribbean countries, too. I'm severing, you hear me, severing, diplomatic relations." Diplomatic relations. That is what any of us in the Diaspora has with these nations we were born in, the ones we live in, and the ones we're supposed to belong to: the most fragile diplomatic relations.

*July 2000, at the corner of Primrose and Davenport*
Here is a new light post. Around it are two newspaper boxes. *The Toronto Star, The Toronto Sun.* Also a wreath and a bouquet of flowers. Somehow, Ma Phoung died here and is missed by family.

*Circa 2000, Associated Press*
*With as many as 2 million women worldwide forced into sexual slavery, the sex trade seems to have replaced narcotics as the favoured illegal trade activity . . . Best estimates show at least 50,000 are brought into the United States annually for forced labour. Feeder countries for the slave trade include*

*Ukraine, Albania, the Philippines, Thailand, Mexico and*
*Nigeria . . . A woman called Inez testified, "We work six days*
*a week and 12 hour days."*

### Circa 1492

The money that financed Columbus's voyage to the
Americas came from a tax which Ferdinand of Aragon and
Isabella of Castille obtained from the church for waging a
"just and holy war" against the Moorish kingdom of
Granada and Islam as a whole. Granada surrendered on
January 2, 1492. Columbus set sail in April 1492.

### 14

On the radio, the CBC, there is a report from the divided
warring city of Mitrovica. The northern part of the city is
Serb, the southern part Albanian. Everyone is determined,
resolute in their hatred for each other. In the background,
in a coffee bar in the north where a Serb is being inter-
viewed, the voice of Ibrahim Ferrer can be heard singing

*De Alto Cedro voy para Marcane*
*Luego a Cueto voy para Mayari*
*El carino que te tengo*
*you no lo puedo negar*
*se me sale la babita*
*yo no lo puedo evitar.*

It is 4:45 a.m. I am doing what I do every time I drink too much wine and wake up suddenly at 4:45 a.m. I read. Eduardo Galeano falls open at this time: "I'm nostalgic for a country which doesn't yet exist on a map." Dear Eduardo, I am not nostalgic. Belonging does not interest me. I had once thought that it did. Until I examined the underpinnings. One is mislead when one looks at the s ails and majesty of tall ships instead of their cargo. But if it were a country where you were my compatriot, then I would reconsider. And think of the things we should have to sort out.

## Maps

I first heard the word *Sargasso* in a history class when I was a child. It described the unending water across which Europeans sailed, bringing people and goods to the Caribbean. The water was supposedly treacherous and sickening, and sailors and ships and cargo were often lost there.

I imagined the Sargasso as tangle — sea tangle — thick as grasses but fluid. I imagined dead sailors, dead ships. I only imagined later dead slaves, suicidal and murdered, strangled again in the grasses of the Sargasso. Then I imagined multitudes, throngs, wandering the bottom of the ocean, eyeless and handless, cuffed and coffled. I would wake up on the point of asphyxiation. Much later my lover had a dream of being cuffed at the ankles. I, watching her sleep, did not know her distress, only lay watching, deciding whether to wake her or let her finish her nightmare. She kicked violently, trying to free herself, cutting my ankle with her toes and waking up to my soothing her. Then I remembered my dreams of the Sargasso, its thick tangle of bones long turned to coral and sand.

## Maps

A rihla is a traveller's account of a pilgrimage. Ibn Jubayr, the foremost practitioner of the form, travelled to Mecca, then through Mesopotamia, Syria, and Sicily, arriving in Granada in 1185. His rihla, written in diary form, contained twenty-seven chapters, one for each month of his journey. It also contained praises to God.

In 1050, an earlier traveller to Mecca, Nasser-e Khosraw, also wrote a diary of his travels, *The Book of Travels*. In it he tells of a figure appearing to him in his sleep, a figure who advised him to seek wisdom. When he asked where wisdom lay, the figure pointed toward Mecca.

## Voyage

The poet André Gide writes in his travel diary *Voyage au Congo et la Retour du Tchad*: "Our travelling companions are mostly officials and traders. I think we are the only ones travelling 'for pleasure.'

"'What are you going out for?'

"'I shall see when I get there.'"

### 1

I am delayed in Frankfurt for four hours. When you are travelling, time is sometimes a pain. You wish to arrive; you are impatient, especially when travelling to Africa. Europe is a nuisance. It is in the way. Yet it is the only way there from here. The waiting area is crowded. It is full of bodies in the middle of long journeys; bodies like mine, tired yet attentive and anticipating. There are bodies, walking, pacing, falling asleep in the waiting room.

My body feels always in the middle of a journey. It is always alert; it does not doze off or sleep easy. When it sleeps, it sleeps like someone expecting an emergency. Waiting is its purpose. It has two speeds, one slow, achingly, the other frenetic, hypervigilant. Under wine or whisky my body can veer toward paralysis or lyric. In Frankfurt these speeds alternate crazily at the thought of going to Africa. Bodies flap in beige and grey coats; black bags are hitched on backs and hips; the air is stale in the waiting room; hundreds are waiting. Sitting, impatient and sluggish, the room is a slow blur. I want to get rid of these people. I want to leave this room and go to Africa.

I am on my way to Johannesburg. It is my first flight to the continent. I will fly over the Door of No Return. I will not go there, but I will feel it somehow. The plane leaves Frankfurt and I sit riveted to the TV screen, which shows a map of Europe and Africa. The symbol of a plane marks our location, as we make our way painstakingly south toward the continent. It is night by the time we take off. Outside the darkness encloses; darkness is the air through which we travel. Moving through dark air or dark water, it is the same. I cannot help thinking, I at least know where I am going. I am going willingly. This electronic map on the TV screen of the plane is not unlike those early maps (which my ancestors probably never saw themselves; they travelled without maps). Perhaps the outline is more accurate, but still only a few cities are filled in — this time for convenience. There is Frankfurt, there Johannesburg, and there Cape Town. There are no places in between, no signs for the physical geography, just an outline. It is as simple as those first maps. It is also a composite of all maps. Its itinerary is all that matters. The time, the kilometres, appear on the screen, well refined now. Why is all geography irony?

The work of watching the map, of tracking the flight to Africa is nerve wracking. We arrive at the coast, Tripoli. We cross Libya and Chad. The rims of my eyes are a burning red. By now the people beside me are asleep. My legs are cramped, my stomach is in a constricted knot. I tell myself to relax, fall asleep. But how can I, crossing Africa? I want to feel it even if I am miles above in the sky, even if I cannot see. I am all nerve and energy at the thought of the great land below. Like all maps, the one on the screen makes the land below seem understandable, as if one could sum up its vastness, its differentiations in a glance, as if one could touch it, hold all its ideas in two hands. I wish I was on the ground. I know I would soon be enveloped by it, overwhelmed as all land overwhelms me. The patience and breadth, even islands overwhelm. The Door of No Return is on my mind. I am crossing the place which holds it; the place which holds the before of history. It is a return, but aptly it is in the air and it is a glancing pass at the Door of No Return. The door is not on this map. The door is on my retina.

## 2

Bangui in the Central African Republic appears when I wake from an open-eyed sleep.

## 3

In 1486 John Afonso of Aveiro reached the kingdom of Benin. My journey is more than eighteen hours long. Down the belly of Africa. Why do I slip into the easy-enough metaphor of Africa as body, as mother? Is it because the door induces sentimentality? The idea of return presumes the certainty of love and healing, redemption and comfort. But this is not return. I am not going anywhere I've been, except in the collective imagination. Yes, the imagination is itself a pliant place, lithe, supple, susceptible to pathos, sympathetic to horror.

## 4

I cannot go back to where I came from. It no longer exists. It should not exist.

When you take a journey, you are no longer yourself. Already no one knows you any more, neither your family nor your friends. The day you decide to leave, the tablecloth seems foreign, the room where you have slept forever seems unfamiliar, as if someone has left it already.

I remember standing at the top of the street to my house when I was thirteen thinking, I will leave here and never return, I am not going to live here. Already the books in my mind were read, already I was forgetting faces and names, already all that was happening had happened. The street was a ghost. I never returned to that street. The house with the hibiscus fence and the butterflies hovering over zinnias. From then on I imagined only.

## 5

Another lidless sleep and we are near Kinshasa. I am looking forward to getting off the plane. It will be the first ground I touch in Africa. It is daylight when we get there, midday really. We left Frankfurt last night and I have not slept. Just before the landing, the pilot announces we will not be allowed to disembark. Political conflict. Fear. Some unrest. The plane lands far away from the terminal. Through the window all I can see is burnt grass. Mobutu Sese Seko is afraid of something or someone.

## 6

André Gide. "I have plunged into this journey like Curtius into the Gulf. I feel already as I had not so much willed it (though for many months past I have been stringing my will up to it) as had it imposed upon me by a sort of ineluctable fatality — like all the important events in my life."

Why would Gide see this voyage as an "ineluctable fatality"? What in his life or culture made it so, made it necessary? Throughout his account I cannot find the answer. Not the answer I need. What was he hoping to find; what was he hoping to think? One travels; one takes oneself intact. With a will. One is a coherent being — needing nothing from the place one travels to but food, shelter, and most importantly that the place one visits appears and in appearance yields a confirming example of one's sentience. Or one travels in disarray, undone, a consciousness formed around displacement, needing nothing that one can put a finger on, needing a centre. And the place is air and burnt grass through a window after eighteen hours of waiting.

7

I don't want to suggest that my thoughts are typical of the Black Diaspora, only that they proceed from the experience. My eyes took in the burnt grass as we sat on the tarmac for another two hours and I wished I could disembark and go to a city, drive along a road with fields and forests on both sides, ramshackle houses and cattle, an oil pipeline silver and dangerous running by, then the city, calamitous and squalling. There in that city or perhaps along the road the ubiquitous Door of No Return would appear.

This opening, which I had hoped to observe, remained compelling though concealed. But why so compelling? Perhaps it is the Holy Grail of the Diaspora. It is the site of pain which will turn into the site of pleasure. Transform us into full being through its immutable knowledge. Transform us into being.

8

By the time we land in Johannesburg I have been in a waking sleep for twenty-four hours. On the drive from the airport I see red land. The land is red here. I remember little else of that journey from the airport to the hotel in Johannesburg. I go to my room. The dead weight of my body hits the small bed. It is afternoon in Johannesburg; the opening of the New Nation Writers Conference will be later that night. Nelson Mandela will be there. It will be a grand welcome and cele-bration. I fall into the deepest of sleeps. I, usually so insom-niac, so fitful, sleep as if forever. I dream. I can't remember what. The next morning I wake up thinking it is still the day before, then realize I have missed the whole evening.

9

Transform us into being. That one door transformed us into bodies emptied of being, bodies emptied of self-interpretation, into which new interpretations could be placed. Phantasm, chimera, vision, Ellison's invisibility. *Spook* is a derogatory description, but it speaks to the psychological arrangements of the describer entering the sign. Entering and occupying the sign. I am, we are, in the Diaspora, bodies occupied, emptied and occupied. If we return to the door it is to retrieve what was left, to look at it — even if it is an old sack, threadbare with time, empty itself of meaning.

## 10

André Gide. "And I come near forgetting that it is nothing but a project made in youth and realized in maturity. I was barely twenty when I first made up my mind to make this journey to the Congo thirty-six years ago."

## 11

Langa. Years ago I had written a poem about this place, never having seen it. It was a poem about state killings of nineteen people at an uprising during apartheid. I had heard about it on the news in Canada. About a town called Uitenhage, the black township outside it called Langa. I had imagined that place and written the poem. Now here I was and the landscape was as I had imagined. Bare, bright reddish-yellow dirt. The people; I noticed their hands, rough, bony, the skin dry and flaky. I noticed eyes like eyes waking up; eyes that were full of tragedy but also eyes that gleamed. It was the most desolate of towns. No, I cannot say that everywhere we went each township seemed as desolate as the other.

The shebeen in Langa is where I end up. It is a simple flat-roofed structure. The beers are served in large brown bottles or large paper cartons. Langa is the kind of place where you want to drink in the middle of the day, perhaps all day long, dreary, such a hot, dry wasteland. It is the place that I imagined; it is the place where events such as have happened would happen.

I remember another shebeen — a rum shop, it's called there — in a village in Dominica. One night some friends and I drive through country darkness, stopped where the car could go no further, and climbed a hill, bumping into tree stumps, arriving at a rum shop. It was not really a shop but a lean-to shack. A man in a ripped merino raised himself from a card game beside the lean-to, slipped behind the makeshift bar, which was a simple piece of wood, and asked us what we wanted. Beer, whisky, he let us go through our urban wishes, then said "nah" to all of them. He only had cask rum, he said. An oily, pungent, potent, uncured extract.

We sat or stood around the one rickety table outside the lean-to and drank this mixture late into the night. A man like the man who just walked into the shebeen in Langa came into the lean-to. He looked a little crazed in the eyes, his hand was bleeding from a cut he seemed to be unaware of. He came toward us, his ragged trousers held up by a bit of twine; he came toward us, a manic smile, a quick walk, his eyes flitting from each of us to the glasses of white liquid in front of us. The man in Langa smiles that same smile. He is dressed in a rough cloth shirt and brown trousers held up by a twisted brown worn belt. He hangs about, staring at us, then buys two large cartons of beer and leaves. He too has a cut on the knuckles of his hand; he too ignores it. Drinking cask rum at the lean-to we tell the bartender to give the man with the manic smile a drink on us. He reluctantly takes the white plastic jug up from the floor, warning us that this man drinks too much, and pours. At the shebeen in Langa I want to find someone for whom I can buy a drink, but generosity would not be sufficient.

This Dominican village was not Langa, but you can understand how you would need to drink in these places. Places where the physical work of collecting each devastating day cakes the body and makes it bleed.

## 12

I had never made up my mind to visit Africa. I had somehow felt the beckoning of the Door of No Return but was prepared to imagine it and never arrive. I have yet to see the door. Cartography is description, not journey. The door, of course, is not on the continent but in the mind; not a physical place — though it is — but a space in the imagination.

## 13

"A sort of ineluctable fatality." What did Gide think would happen to him in the Congo? Perhaps he had read Conrad; he must have known of the brutalities of Leopold. What insights did he think he could draw? Was the Congo/Africa some sort of "holy" grail for European men of his time? A touchstone to their existence, an abyss whose gaze they were compelled to meet. And why Africa? In all the things I've read I cannot fathom it. The economics, the material power — all that I know and understand — but the perverse spiritual fascination, the "sort of ineluctable fatality" — the reasons must be situated in the self-interpretations, which I do not have access to or can only glimpse through power.

## 14

Willie Kgotsitsile greets me in Johannesburg as if he knows me. His face is joyful, mischievous. He says, "I have been waiting to meet you." He is a poet and we meet as poets. "Marlene told me about you," he says, "so we have met before." Willie is glowing. His smile, his whole body is incandescent. I am meeting him at the end of apartheid. He greets me as someone coming out of the end of a great and long tunnel. But he is not weighed down; he is buoyant.

## Maps

I run each morning, two, three, sometimes four kilometres. Part of March, all of April, all of May. I can't run five. I am eating up kilometres on my way to where it is always twilight. I am running out of the world.

## The Man from the Oldest City in the World

### 1

I am hurrying to the PEN benefit. I am to read there. Something from Neruda; his letter to another writer. "Miguel Otero Silva, In Caracas." It is a letter, a poem about his choices for poetry, about finding poetry not "occupied exclusively with metaphysical subjects."

"Life is like the sky, Miguel, when we put/loving and fighting in it, words that are bread and wine."

I swing into the parking lot at King and John streets. The evening is glistening after a shower of rain, car lights reflect off the wet streets. A slight thin drizzle is still falling. There, near the SkyDome, near the theatres, there glitters the great building of the CBC from which the national culture emanates across the country — incessant, repetitive European classical music, deracinated jazz tucked away at night, waxy talk so careful, so nervous. Across the street is the theatre where the benefit will be held. I am going to a room, a theatre, full of writers. Writers like me and not like me. Shining escalators, velvet drapes, and soft carpeting will greet me. I seal myself in the cylinder of black pants, black jacket, green shawl. I'm thinking of Neruda and this letter to a friend. Each time I walk through these kinds of halls I must summon the writers I feed on and in whom I find comradeship. Today, today it is Neruda.

> *I took life*
> *and I faced her and kissed her,*
> *and then went through the tunnels of the mines*
> *to see how other men live.*
> *And when I came out, my hands stained with garbage*
>    *and sadness*
> *I held my hands up and showed them to the generals,*
> *and said: "I am not a part of this crime."*
> *. . . I had brought joy over to my side.*

It is fifty years after Neruda wrote this letter and I clasp it when I lose my way because it is as if he has written it to me; it is my faith that Neruda can write a poem fifty years ago and I can feel its company now.

## 2

There is a city here where I walk to see how others live. I could, I suppose, see about myself only. I could be unaffected. I could come to the easy belief that, really, what is there to speak against? I could develop that voice so full of cold address to beauty. I could with some self-defacement go about the business of making my living. I could say in that way that many do: oh, it's not so bad, your writing need not show your skin, it need not speak of trouble, history is a burden after all. But Neruda summons me, is waiting for me at the end of every sentence. I cannot ignore my hands "stained with garbage and sadness."

## 3

What holds poetry together in this city, what holds me together, is the knowledge that I cannot resist seeing; what holds me is the real look of things. If I see someone I see the ghost of them, the air around them, and where they've been. If I see the city I see its living ghostliness — the stray looks, the dying hands. I see its needs and its discomforts locked in apartments, its time that no one has — the growing citizenry of homelessness — the man sitting on the corner of Bathurst and College panhandling, saying, "Have a nice day, have a very nice day" to anyone and everyone; the woman who used to be a girl, when I was a girl, and she French just from Quebec City, now bloated on bad food and sleeping variously at Spadina and Bloor, at College and Spadina. I remember her as a flower child, wearing a thin Indian cotton dress, her hair on her narrow shoulders. She is still upbeat as then, bubbly but sometimes disoriented. The man who walks back and forth pacing the pavement on Shuter Street near the park as if he is waiting for someone; or the woman pacing and preaching at St. Clair and Oakwood in a language misunderstood as broken but sustaining its own logic of imprecations. These are people on the edges of the city, some would say, not emblematic. I know they might be the edges and easily ignored, but they curl into the middle. The middle of the city, where what looks like an ordinary life is composed of what is beaten into or calculated and chalked up to the world. What is accepted with a shrug but erodes the soul, burns it like so much acid. We'll go around again, they say, we admit, we confess to not being fit for your world. The exhaustion of it.

4

I have crumpled Neruda in my hand to visit this room because I think it is difficult to see here in this city; no one wants to see, or seeing is a charity they submit to. Everything far away is visible; everything close is viewed with distrust or disbelief, is viewed as imaginary.

*Have you ever spent a whole day close to sea birds*
*watching how they fly? they seem*
*to be carrying the letters of the world to their destinations.*

## 5

I park my Jeep, smiling at the attendant, asking him,
"Where?" The lot seems full. I point at him, pleading,
asking, "Where?" Give me a break, I'm late, find me a spot,
please. He is high cheekboned, all almond-shaped eyes, all
tight Ethiopian black curls, slender. I say, give me a break,
bro — reaching for a language from another time which he
and I now share, our common language. He gestures to a
spot. I quickly fill it, then lock the Jeep and speed toward
him with my keys and money. He says, "No keys, it's fine."
He takes the money. I ask him, "What's happening?" smiling, needing to leave quickly anyway, my question only to
preserve the thin camaraderie of the Diaspora; really, only
to speed him. He says calmly, "Look," gesturing with his
languid hand, "Look, I come from one of the oldest cities
in the world. The oldest civilization. They build a parking
lot and they think that it is a civilization." Stunned, I burst
out laughing. And he joins me. We laugh and laugh and I
reply, "True, true." "The oldest civilization," he says again.
"True," I repeat. I don't care if I am late now. Neruda's letter
is in my hand, and this man's words are in my head.

*nothing they can do*
*but rent a room across the street, and tail us*
*so they can learn to laugh and cry like us.*

———————

The city is a labyrinth of grim hurts and sweet ironies. Former citizens of old cities, failed translators of ideologies, speechless interlocutors of inexpressible feeling.

It is Monday morning, 9 a.m., at the courthouse on Jarvis Street. To get into the courthouse one has to go through the obligatory metal detector and pass by several policemen. Even though one is merely an observer one cannot help but feel an immediate loss of control and a sense of surveillance. The crowd standing outside waiting for the doors to open is mostly young . . . children. Here, they are called juveniles. They are anywhere from eleven to seventeen years old. They all look eight. Some of them are trying to look older, tougher. Some of them are scared. Most are alone, some with a grim-faced mother or grandmother. Some are smoking cigarettes nonchalantly. They are grouped in little packs, those of them without mothers or grandmothers, trying to appear unperturbed. But perhaps they are unperturbed; some of them are veterans. The doors open and we all troop in through the turnstiles and the metal detectors.

The corridors and vestibules fill up; there aren't enough seats in Courtroom No. 1 for the crowd. A policewoman stands at the door of the courtroom. She answers a few questions from those who don't know the rules. Most wait. She looks as if she thinks all of it wearisome — so do many of the children. They are urban children — cool and bored is their emotional attire. Baggy pants worn below the hips, underwear showing, skin-tight pants, belly buttons pierced; hair frosted, streaked, one curl down the side of the forehead; baseball caps — this is the outer attire, affecting that same cool, bored, knowledgeable-beyond-their-years look. And perhaps they *are* cool, bored, knowledgeable beyond their years. I don't know. A city can do that. The doors to Courtroom No. 1 open. The crowd walks in, filling the seats. The policewoman, joined by a policeman, instructs boys to take off their caps. We stand as the judge enters. Two court clerks sit below him to his right. They are Black women, one older, one younger, one in glasses. The judge is not formidable as one imagines judges. He is white. The Crown attorney and the legal aid attorneys look weary, and it's only 9:30 or so. They obviously know each other; they decide some dates, drop into the legal talk, settle what to do with the defendants. It is a routine they practise each day. They could probably do this asleep. As each case is called and a date is set or postponed the children walk to the middle of the courtroom, stand, then are instructed to go to the clerks, where they are given a pink piece of paper with a new date. The charges aren't read out; this is only a court for setting dates and issuing warrants for those who haven't appeared. Before the judge arrived, six or so teenagers in cuffs were brought up from the holding area downstairs. They affect an even more bored look, glazed really. They've been in custody. They are either heroes or scarecrows to the other teenagers in the room. One by one names are called and I see the children at first tentatively stand, knees weak, and make their way the ten feet or so to the bar. Something curious happens to most of them in their walk up the aisle. They transform from scared and teary to bold and accomplished, as if this is routine, as if they did this yesterday. I see their backs straighten and their heads lift from shame to insolent dignity. Inside they're making some decision — some resistance — "this is what I am then." Something else is noticeable in Courtroom No. 1. The defendants are Chinese, Hispanic, Portuguese, Italian, African/Caribbean, Vietnamese, Russian. But not really. None of them know these origins except through their parents or grandparents. They were all born in this city. Some are a mix of a few of those specifics, some are co-defendants across those specifics. As they go up one by one to collect the pink sheets of paper, emotions changing now from insolent dignity to ennui, the clerks who seem Caribbean in origin give each child a look of reprimand, as if they're disappointed in this bunch of children who have wasted their parents' sacrifice. They look at these children like disgusted relatives, aunts who are fed up with bad behaviour. The bleached-blond Chinese boy, the red-streaked Indian girl take on these looks and swagger off, smirking, out of the courtroom. Three young women saunter up the aisle as their names are called. Candace Premdass, Stacy Zeballos, and June Nguyen. Candace Premdass is wearing a Catholic girls' school uniform, the plaid skirt hiked up to mid-thigh, blue calf socks, platform shoes. Stacy Zeballos is in a baggy sweatshirt; June Nguyen is wraithlike in bell-bottoms. Their transatlantic names are the mystery of this city, its hybridization. Candace Premdass, Stacey Zeballos, June Nguyen. They walk lazily toward the judge. "See what you can do with us," they seem to say, "deal with this." Candace and Premdass, Stacy and Zeballos, June and Nguyen. Other and other. How did they all get together, I wonder. Not just their first and last names but the three of them. Friends, co-conspirators, co-defendants. They met as outsiders, no doubt. Outsiders to the city and outsiders in their own homes; the homes, the families that gave them the last names, the same families that gave them the first names to protect them from the last names. What they did isn't clear: shoplifting, perhaps; fighting three other girls, perhaps. Anyway, three of them did whatever it was together. Candace has a swagger; June has a supermodel runway walk — she's the tallest; Stacey is the only one who looks mildly nervous. She stands between the other two. They keep each other company in the desolate courtroom in the desolate city, this transatlantic space trio. But those are my words, my sentiments. For them, the city is beautiful and reckless, a roller coaster of laughter and lipstick, of talking and dissing and high-fiving and wide eyes of mock offence and wonder, of rap music and boys they cruise, and of just, well, cool. This courtroom is a rite of passage for these diasporic children; they would give up their lives like the boys in cuffs behind the Plexiglas with the guard from Mimico, just as soon as they will saunter out of Courtroom No. 1, relieved, and in the hallway giggle about how awesome it was. A date is set and they approach the two clerks, who give them each a reproachful look. The one giving out the pink slips puts them down on the bar, refusing to hand them to the girls. Candace Premdass snatches her paper, her posse right after her, and leaves the courtroom rolling her eyes in exasperation.

———

In this parking lot of a civilization I meet a girl with a murmurous baby at the Mimico Youth Detention. She is waiting to see her boyfriend. She knows the ropes: she tells me where to put my ID for the guard, she tells me what noises mean, she tells me where to sit, she says the baby resembles her boyfriend inside. The baby's going to be tall like him. She hopes he knows he has to stop this, the boy is inside for possession. He can't be around bad people, she says, and not expect to get in trouble, too. She sounds like she's fifty. She's seventeen. So's the boy she's waiting on. She's finishing high school; she wants a Jeep like mine. After we each finish our hour behind Plexiglas talking to the boys we know in detention there, making conversation we each try to infuse with a sense of the boys we knew on the outside — she perhaps accomplishing this better than I, she's younger — I give her a ride to the subway. She was, she wants . . . I can feel a never-going-to-be-sated hunger there.

We, she and I, move in this normal world of jail and babies and wants, thinking nothing of cumbersome baby strollers and teenage mothers in high school. Our families are full of rap musicians and basketball dunking champions, runners and comedians who father children, give up chances, make babies instead, live in leaky Ontario housing projects, hang themselves or take pills and leave their bodies for even more tragic aunts, uncles, and sisters to find floating in bathtubs. She and I live in the living of it.

> *What happiness, Miguel!*
> *Are you going to ask where I am?*
> *I'll tell you — giving only details useful to the state.*

Here, Neruda, it is as if poetry does not matter. The state does not have to look for us. We walk to their building, give them our wrists upheld. Muriel Rukeyser knew it, too. She said, "They say there is no penalty for poets,/ There is no penalty for writing poems./ They say this. This is the penalty."

———————

The man from the oldest city in the world and I are shaking with laughter. Then I walk toward the theatre. Its glittering glass doors, its self-conscious newness, its disposable modernity. Years ago it, too, was a parking lot; in another decade it will become one. Around me is the parking lot, the great parking lot temporarily occupied by buildings. This is what he looks out on every day, his curly head shaking. He is fitted into a box four feet or so by four feet in the middle of it. In the winter he has a heater. I imagine him on those ash-cold days beginning the desolate night shift, surveying "their" civilization. He himself has arrived at the parking lot probably spilled up by a war, lucky enough to have escaped it. Brooding over the parking lot he thinks of this chance, some mishap or fortune now indistinguishable, which has landed him here. He lives somewhere in the place called the "jungle" at Lawrence and Bathurst, or in the highrises at Kipling and Dixon, but he spends most of these days in this unending parking lot, which is the sum of its civilization, laughing sardonically at himself and waiting for a woman in a hurry to listen to his joke. I do not come from any old city. My civilization is the parking lot, but for a moment I recognize the attendant's "they." It is a grim laughter we share. Yes, it is at the ironic circumstances of belonging to this civilization of parking lots. I am the citizen of the parking lot.

———————

So much goes on in this city. Somewhere among its millions of people someone is sitting in a four-foot-square box and thinking about an older city, thinking, "They build a parking lot and they think that it is a civilization." He is shaking his head at his own predicament and laughing to himself. Someone else is walking toward a theatre, a concert hall, with the cadence of Neruda's letter in her head, and a joke from the man from the oldest city in the world. Somehow she is comforted by this joke, somehow it helps her make it across the street and into the concert hall, it makes her walk to the podium and read Neruda's letter with all the more certainty that there's a country with an old city and a letter.

## Ossington to Christie, Toronto

In a new city there are ghosts of old cities. There are lies and re-creations. Everyone thinks that a city is full of hope, but it isn't. Sometimes it is the end of imagination. It is where everyone comes to put a stop to the hard things in life and to become perfect. Those who are born there think they know perfection. What they know is useless after one hundred miles, unless in another city. But this uselessness humbles ghosts. Ghosts try to step into life. Selam Restaurant, Jeonghysa Buddhist Temple, Oneda's Market, West Indian and Latin American Foods, Afro Sound, Lalibela Ethiopian Cuisine, Longo's Vegetable and Fruits, Astoria Athens Restaurant, Coffee Time, Star Falafel, Vince Gasparos Meats, Eagle Travel, Taygetos Café and Greek Social Club, Pathfinder Bookstore, African Wings Travel, DEC Bookroom and Centre for Social Justice, PCI House–Internet Café, Khosla Travel, Greek Credit Union, Menalon, Asmaria Restaurant and Bar, Turkish Restaurant, Café Jose, African Paradise, Sawa, Manolito Bar Café, Wing Po Variety, El Jaroleto Restaurant, Ramon Humeres — Dentist, Universal Beauty Supply.


## Beat


### 1

I sat in a dark smoke-filled bar in New York City wearing a black turtleneck sweater, black jeans, and black boots. My hair was cut in a sharp pageboy, my eyebrows were plucked to arrows. I sat there thinking this thought: Journeys are perhaps always imaginary. This bar was filled with others like me, smoking cigarettes and drinking. We were listening intently (yet languidly) to poets like us who stood in a small spotlight declaiming on the ache in human beings. I snapped my fingers in appreciation, murmuring "cool" when some profound thought had been expressed. My hair formed a soft halo in the spotlight as I too rose to speak a glimmer of wisdom into the urban void. The bar, dark and spectral with smoke and enlightenment, snapped its approval. Then Ginsberg walked in and read "Howl" for the first time. Journeys are always imaginary.

I was twelve and sitting in Miss Sirju's English class. Miss Sirju called me Deanne and insisted that I answer to this name, which I had never been called but which a careless registry clerk had attached to my birth certificate when an aunt had gone to the Mayaro registry, some miles away from Guayguayare, where I was born, to register my birth. This clerk had not bothered to listen closely to my aunt or had thought my aunt's opinion on the matter of my name worthless. My aunt, I don't know which one of them, I don't even know if it was an aunt, my aunt did not look at the birth certificate, nor did anyone else in my family, nor did anyone else in any school administration or church or neighbourhood or playground until Miss Sirju, my first form mistress. Not Miss Greenidge, my fastidious ABC dame school teacher; not Miss James, my primary school headmistress; not Miss Palmer, my standard one teacher, who would have had a perfect right to investigate me had she caught me cheating at poetry recital; not even Miss Meighu, my high school principal. None of these authorities had challenged the name my family had called me since I was born. None of them had questioned my authenticity or my identity until Miss Sirju, who decided to teach me my real name when I was twelve years old.

The transformation into the girl Miss Sirju called Deanne was distasteful to me even though there were many girls I had read of whom I was willing to embody. The girls in *Little Women*, for example, or the girls in Enid Blyton mysteries, or the girl in "Oh Mary, go and call the cattle home." But this Deanne seemed to be a girl without a story. When Miss Sirju called Deanne, I did not answer. I was not being wilful. I looked around like all the other girls waiting for this Deanne to answer. Soon enough the other girls looked at me as if the word *Deanne* were an accusation. Miss Sirju gave me a bad conduct mark for being rude and ignoring her when she called "Deanne." She somehow did not understand that I did not hear my name, my name not being Deanne, and therefore could not answer. Her class became a torture chamber for me. Some days I remembered her problem and answered just to keep the peace. Some days I forgot this obsession of hers, my mind on my own life and not any fiction of Miss Sirju's. On the days that I remembered her problem, she played a cat and mouse game with me. After calling "Deanne" once, which I answered to when I was alert, she would call "Deanne" again unexpectedly to catch me out. Miss Sirju's English class was therefore a painful place. I could not concentrate on William Wordsworth or William Makepeace Thackeray, who were definitely Williams and never had to endure someone like Miss Sirju, I'd wager. So in order therefore to transcend Miss Sirju, I sat in a dark smoke-filled bar in New York City wearing a black turtleneck sweater, waiting to stand in the natural halo of my hair preceding Ginsberg's "Howl."

I had arrived at the bar following various pieces of information as to its whereabouts. A magazine, an arts report on the radio, a reading of a poem, a novel set in New York City, a piece of jazz heard on Radio Antilles, a glimpse over a shoulder at a neighbour's television set of people calling themselves beatniks. These led me to the bar, down the steps of a New York brownstone, a brownstone such as the one Paule Marshall described in *Brown Girl, Brownstones*, describing a girl such as me living in New York City. Down the steps of this brownstone with a blue light small in its window on any evening there could be music — a solo saxophonist or a guitarist. I also played the guitar from time to time in this bar. Sometimes a singer with a plaintive voice would sing. On any evening there could be extemporizing on the nature of life and the world; on any evening, pulling a menthol through my lungs, I could obtain cool — a oneness with the hard city and the uninvolved universe.

## 2

When you embark on a journey, you have already arrived. The world you are going to is already in your head. You have already walked in it, eaten in it; you have already made friends; a lover is already waiting.

When I arrived at the apartment on Keele Street, Toronto, I was in America. Somewhere downtown was the hip fast world of jazz and poetry, esoteric arguments and utopian ideas. I had sat for six hours on the airplane, excited, air sick and afraid. Up the Atlantic, perhaps over the Bahamas, my resolve had dwindled, my plans had been thrown into crisis. America had seemed too big an idea for me. I felt small; who was I to plan such a journey? I felt presumptuous, forward, putting myself on this plane and believing that I could arrive anywhere that would require my presence. I was not used to the buffeting of air against steel, the slightest movement made me queasy. And just as a weak person would betray a cause, I felt like turning back. Of course, thankfully I had no control of the plane so I sat it out, not because I had not weakened but because I had no choice. What in fact was I to return to? A dreadful house, a dubious future, an alienated present. I had made no friendships that I could sustain, no friendships that take one through life — friendships for me were a burden. I had been distracted the moment I heard the faraway BBC voice beckoning me; I had become dissociated the moment I had read *Jane Eyre*, the moment I had played Portia in the *Merchant of Venice*, the moment I had pranced about my high school stage as King Herod. The very moment I had walked onto the stage of the Naparima Bowl and recited, "No one was in the field but Polly Flint and me" from a poem I do not recall. I had been snatched away by James Baldwin, first to Harlem and then to Paris. So here I was on a plane, and my body felt weak and incapable. My plan to get to America now seemed shaky, as tendrilled as the sky outside, which I now could not look at. I regretted the window seat. It startled me that a little physical discomfort, a small inconvenience surely, would make me want to turn back. How was I going to handle the large inconveniences, the demonstrations, the sit-ins, the jailings I had planned to be part of when I arrived? But even in this depth, back was nowhere. Forward, if I did not die of fear, was America.

So when I arrived at the sixteenth-floor apartment in the west end of Toronto, I was relieved. I was in America.

America was a world already conceived in my mind, long before I set foot in that apartment, long before I ever saw it. In fact, when I saw it I did not see it; I saw what I had imagined. One knows where one is going before one arrives. The map is in your head. You merely have to begin moving to have it confirmed. My city was a city busy with people, with purposes. It was inhabited by lye-slick-haired dudes, as in Malcolm X's autobiography; there were dashikied cadres as in don lee's poem "But he was cool." Mothers like Paule Marshall's, little girls like Toni Cade Bambara's, protesters at snack counters and on buses heading south, militants on courthouse steps with rifles. All the inhabitants of this city in America were African-American. I was prepared to speak on Nina Simone's "Mississippi God damn" and Trane's "Afro Blue." I was longing to sit someplace and listen to James Baldwin warn of the fire the next time. Owusu Saduki was to come from Buffalo to speak in my city. I was already living in my city long before boarding the air-sickening jet to make the journey. The plane landed in Canada, but I was in America. I had come to meet my compatriots at the barricades, to face the dogs and the water hoses of Bull Connors, to defy George Wallace. These moments were my city.

3

In a newspaper in another country, any country is a monograph of energetic and elliptical dispatches. This I had taken note of while discoursing my way along latitudes of newsprint, making a compendium of the salient points. In fact, I had memorized the monograph itself — the streets it sketched, the particular contours, the landmarks. So when I embarked, I was already its citizen. I was dressed in a leatherette suit, approximating as well as I could under the circumstances the iconography of a woman in my situation, my hair was bursting from its orthodox perm, my family was already not my family, my road was already laid down. My city was a city in my imagination where someone suddenly and plainly appears as if belonging and not belonging, where someone may disappear also into nothing or everything. When I landed in Toronto I put my luggage down in the apartment on Keele Street and headed for Harlem, the Apollo, 125th Street.

4

I stepped into the cool opening of the Door of No Return. My feet landed where my thoughts were. This is the trick of the door — to step through and be where you want to be. Our ancestors were bewildered because they had a sense of origins — some country, some village, some family where they belonged and from which they were rent. We, on the other hand, have no such immediate sense of belonging, only of drift.

## Maps

Isabella of Castille commissioned a polyptych altarpiece in 1496. Juan de Flandes and Michel Sittow were retained to work on the miniature altarpiece. In one panel called "The Multiplication of the Loaves and Fishes," Isabella and Ferdinand are inserted into the scene at the front of the crowd near Jesus Christ. Isabella is kneeling; Ferdinand is standing.

What can be inferred here is that Isabella led a fabulous religious fantasy life. To see herself and Ferdinand at this occasion attests to the fertility of her imagination. But perhaps it was Juan de Flandes' attempt to ingratiate himself further with Isabella of Castille; perhaps he said to her one day, "Dearest Queen, this scene would be nothing without you. You simply must be in it." Then again, the idea of multiplying loaves and fishes, this particular miracle, must have appealed to Isabella as she and Ferdinand acquired more and more wealth.

## Copper

My uncle used to work copper. He was a tall dark man. His face was beautiful and chiselled, as chiselled as the scars that cut into the auburn face of the sheet of copper. His teeth were white and even in his sculpted jaw; he grinned easily. Just as easily he took a smile back, his face turning stern in admonition of some small weakness of nieces and nephews like a stolen mango or a too lazy Sunday when the shoes weren't whitened. But my uncle used to work copper. With screwdriver, knife, pick, and hammer, he would chisel and pound some image out of the flat surface of a sheet of copper. He worked from no photograph or drawing but from a pattern he must have had inside himself. A mask emerged which at the time, having no other words for it, we called African — serene eyes, broad nose, full lips — not a recognizable face but an image, a presentiment of a face. This face came out of my uncle. My uncle was a teacher. He wore dark trousers and starched white long-sleeved shirts to go to his job as a teacher. He spoke and enforced proper English in our house and in his classrooms like he beat out African masks from copper. My second uncle wore these masks from copper. My second uncle wore these masks on carnival day — sometimes as breastplates or headdresses on whatever 'mas he was playing. My first uncle never played 'mas. He only coaxed the face out of the blank sheet of copper. Over months he would pick and mark, beat and drum out whatever spirit lay there. Eyes, jaws, cheeks, foreheads would emerge.

Scarifications mirrored in scarifications — the ones my uncle made of the ones on the face of the image. My uncle's hands were deft, his fingers black on the back of his hands, pink on the flat of his palms. The other uncle would wear this mask on his chest or his forehead surrounded by feathers and beads and dance under the burning sun — singing nonsensical chants that stood for African or Amerindian words.

My uncle would take months to draw and cut out the masks; he would leave it for days, frustrated that a cheekbone would not level out. My uncle was not a scholar of African art of any kind. He did not know of the personal masks of the Bassa people, he did not know of the men's society masks of the Manding people or Guinea, nor the dance mask of the Igbo or the Bawa or Bamana people. He had no recall of the Baule, the Oan, the Mossi, the Ogoni, the Sennefo, the Ngbaka, or the Akwaya. My uncle only had the gaping Door of No Return, a memory resembling a memory of a thing that he remembered. And not so much remembered as felt. And not so much felt as a memory which held him.

He beat these masks out of himself every afternoon after he came home from school. What happened at school we did not know. What happened to make him search the copper face of the metal hoping for and drilling an image of a self he suspected lay in him. And he oriented that self to Africa. What made him appear at seven in the morning, a conservative young man, dutiful to his family, dressed in dark pants and white shirt, a white handkerchief to sop his forehead in the early brilliant sun, peeking evenly out of his back pocket, his shoes black and shiny, the crease in his trousers razor sharp. Then after school his chest bare, his mouth slightly open, his tongue emphasizing his hands beating and burnishing the metal face, brightly, brilliantly copper.

My second uncle had no such reserve to beat out. He was an electrician; he went to work as he liked, played 'mas, drank, ran women and card games; he was always looking for an angle. He had no discipline, as his parents said, nothing out of which to beat copper into an African face. So he made 'mas all the time. His only discipline were his mother and father but my first uncle's discipline was larger. He was trying to become someone. Which meant to be a schoolteacher or better. Which meant to lead a respectful life, an exemplary life — a life which negated the effects of the Door of No Return — to be lifted above the stereotype of "uncivilized." Not an ordinary life, not a life that was simple, but a life always dedicated to self-conscious goodness, self-conscious excellence.

My first uncle also carved wood. He carved a profile of a man, sometimes a woman, the cheekbone high, the eye serene, the lips full, the jaw strong. He carved this profile in wood, polished it black and smooth. He carved this profile over and over again. When I was small the house seemed full of jet black heads, smooth and shiny, their foreheads serene as if looking down on some land, some jewel, some thing they owned and were happy with. These heads were as serene as my uncle's coppers were ferocious. In the burning carnival sun, laying on my second uncle's chest or over his brow, my first uncle's copper masks shone to blinding. My first uncle did not go to 'mas; he stayed home, sending instead his ferocious copper into the street battling the sun itself. His will and what was inside him screamed brilliantly over San Fernando. Dancing along, stopping to inspire awe and fear, my uncle's copper masks visited these faraway streets as emissaries, spirits from a lost place. In our house my uncle carved his serene profiles, which he never felt complete enough, over and over again.

How he must have felt. That he could not perfect serenity. He would walk around the house carving and smoothing. He would pick up one wooden face, shine it for an hour or so, finding a spot he loved, then another, smoothing the brow, glossing the cheekbone.

My uncle moved to Canada later. First to Hamilton, then to Toronto, and then to Sudbury. I do not know where his passions went then. I do not think that his hand carved any more wood or beat out any more metal. Steel and nickel parenthesized him. I do not know what he thought of that town, Hamilton, wreathed in deadly smoke and steel rust; I do not know what he thought of the equally toxic frozen smoke of Sudbury, the slag heaps close to his house, the dominant brown rock that seemed to dull every sound, every echo there. I do not know what became of him, the fierce him he tried to carve — he tried to calm to serenity. I suspect that he was drowned the way one drowns, often willingly, in any metropole. The city drowns out your longings and your fears, replacing them with its own anonymous desire. These three cities in the northern hemisphere took him to the more mundane vulgar acts of acquisition, away from any contemplation of the self into the hurly-burly of a packaged life, property and consumption. And he may have been grateful.

## More Maps

According to my uncle the world was its books, its words, its languages. His evenings of grammar drills induced illnesses, panic attacks, nausea, and sleepiness. "'It' could never 'have,'" he would shout to some child saying, "Uncle, it have a man outside asking for you." "'There is,' 'there are' for the plural, but 'it' could never 'have.'" No simple request or statement went without such correction, until this child forgot or regretted what he or she wanted. Soon there was pure silence around my uncle.

What is the Spanish word for butter? *Mantequilla.* What is the Spanish word for bread? *Pan.* What is the Spanish word for butterfly? *Mariposa.* Girl? *Niña.* Water? *Agua.* Beach? *Playa.* And for dreams? *Suenos.* Hope? *Esperanza.* Help? *Socorro.* Sometimes this child would discover quite by mistake his or her own hopeless desire for *esperanza, socorro, suenos* against this endless schooling.

Out of the blue my uncle's face turning from laughter to seriousness would say, "Conjugate the verb *tener.*" Just as he was teaching you the waltz by having you step on his feet as he danced to Pete d'Ulyut's Band playing "Stardust," he would surprise you with the difficult declension of the verb *llevar.*

## Conjugations in Disgrace and Paradise

Well, I suppose then, my uncle taught me to hang on to the world from the arms of books, or words at any rate. To be alert to translation even as your feet dance. Even if "Stardust" is playing, or "Via Con Dios, My Darling," one must be alert to questions of meaning that may be lying in ambush or bearing down on you, or lurking in the soft recesses of the livingroom like your beautiful schoolteacher uncle. To read is to traverse the limnal space between laughter and spelling, between syntax and dancing.

So I am on a plane going to Australia, reading J.M. Coetzee's novel *Disgrace*. It is his only novel where one can clearly read race as its subject. His earlier books seemed to refuse race. Who could blame him? Since South Africa reduced human beings to its arbitrary biological tyranny, for a writer working under the totalitarian state of apartheid, allegory was an obvious literary strategy. A way of surviving apartheid's ruthless violence. The victory over apartheid seemed to free Coetzee to realism, to more plain terms about race. That moment must have been odd — stunning, euphoric. When the world changes, even when it is the change you have longed for and dreamed, it must be destabilizing. It turned Coetzee's style from allegory to a kind of journalism.

As I read *Disgrace*, these thoughts come to me. Writers do not lead, they follow, however prescient their works might seem at times. It is only that they, unlike most people, cannot shut up. They gush out what they see — whatever thought they have, and everyone around them is startled because they've said what everyone's been thinking. Sometimes they see too early, sometimes too late. Sometime they gush their fears, and then sometimes they blurt out their affinities.

To enter Coetzee's earlier work was to enter that odd trope, the "universal," the "human." At least some of us could. Others of us who saw a less noble and more vulgar world may have been untouched. Or may have, being more cynical, read that trope as "white"; or may have read the helplessness of his characters as luxury and, more telling, may have read his characters' inaction as hardly remarkable. I for one always felt a slight discomfort in his texts even though I longed for inclusion in his "human." As I had yearned decades before to dance with my uncle but had dreaded his jolting conjugations. For me, Coetzee's narratives, for all their universality, could not contest or enlighten the other narratives emanating from South Africa. I mean the crowds of demonstrators being shot by deadly bullets or whipped with *sjamboks*, the desert-like hunger of townships, the imprisonments, the detainees being thrown from multi-storied police buildings, the physical tortures, the political prisoners whose bodies were braced in the eloquent language of resistance. Perhaps the "universal" could not compete or respond to this din of narrations. Himself freed of the trope in post-apartheid South Africa, the results in Coetzee's novel *Disgrace* are startling and revealing.

On the plane to Australia, traversing Coetzee's South Africa, Toni Morrison's *Paradise* limns on the horizon. These two, *Disgrace* and *Paradise*, seem to be in conversation with each other. At least now in my mind. Writing is, after all, an open conversation. Works find each other. They live in the same world. The narrative of race is embedded in all narratives. My uncle loved James Baldwin at the same time he loved Lawrence Durrell. At once he cut his hair and dressed like Sam Cooke, then he enforced the proper use of English and berated the use of the demotic. So you see, reading is full of complications.

To enter Toni Morrison's fiction is to enter her rewriting of the myth of America, and so it is also a conversation about grace, redemption, and that quintessential American ideal, happiness. Against the official American narrative, Morrison narrates the African-American presence that underpins the official story but is rarely, truly braided among the narratives of the "pilgrims," the "founding fathers," the "west," and so on.

In a society so invested in its "inherent goodness" and moral superiority, Morrison's voice is always trenchant. Her project to write myth is nothing less than trying to take command of that national narrative — to call it to account for the injustice it elides. Her language is biblical the way the Bible is more than story but narrative, more than narrative myth-wide in its reach of event and meaning. Yet within all that grand beauty is a palpable disillusion, an inexorable tragedy. Myth is of course seductive, but it needs material power to enforce it. The dominant myth overwhelms Morrison's mythmaking, leaving her characters stranded in a kind of inevitable failure. In history. The daily bulletins on Black America seen through mass media encroach on the space of Morrison's narratives. She cannot write fast enough to counter them. In *Paradise*, Morrison's voice is finally sepulchral. As if having offered America Genesis she now curses it with Revelations.

Any representation of blackness interests me. Coetzee's English professor Lurie, is on a collision course with blackness however obtuse. When he is charged by a student with sexual harassment, Coetzee slyly brings him before a committee of inquiry. One cannot help but draw the parallel between this committee of inquiry and the Truth and Reconciliation Committee in South Africa. I notice that Coetzee awkwardly collapses the so-called "political correctness" of feminism with that of post-apartheid "black rule." The committee of inquiry is racially marked by their names revealing a strange assortment of "modern" and ascendant interests — Blacks, Asians, aspiring women and a token holdover from the past. Significantly the chair of the committee is a Professor of Religious Studies (shades of Desmond Tutu).

A cunning voice from my childhood living room asks if anyone else notices all this interpolation and what it might mean.

I recall one character in *Paradise* saying "Slavery is our past. Nothing can change that, certainly not Africa." Another answers too feebly perhaps against this weighty legacy, "We live in the world, Pat. The whole world." Morrison's America is the painful void of the Diaspora. *Paradise* is about the nature of blackness. When the novel begins in the 1960s these debates are at a height in Ruby and they have found a focus in a nearby unconventional convent of stray and destitute women. The first chapter starts with the murders by the men of Ruby of women in the convent. It reads provocatively, "They kill the white girl first."

As if *Paradise* and *Disgrace* were a call and answer chant, blackness and whiteness angle and parry perilously. Everyone else is asleep on the plane to Australia when Lurie is read the charges against him. He replies "I am sure the members of this committee have better things to do with their time than rehash a story over which there will be no dispute. I plead guilty to both charges. Pass sentence, and let us get on with our lives." He refuses repentance or contrition. It is probably true, I think as I stretch my body across four seats in the middle aisle, that repentance or contrition or a going over of the story or even any attempts at the truth may not be sufficient for the atrocities of apartheid. I have a mind that these may be the preoccupations of victims. The "why" that wracks them even more than the "who."

Lurie rather dramatically compares the committee's procedures to Mao's China with its "recantation, self-criticism, public apology." So it seems that *Disgrace* rejects a communal remedy or any possibility of change. And this is where I find the novel ultimately pessimistic. Because Coetzee doesn't offer any other choices except death. Lurie's movement to some understanding about his place in the universe only comes through the work he begins doing in a clinic that euthanizes stray dogs and cats. It is ironic that he cannot find the same fealty for the human beings he encounters. Allegory again? And again the daily narratives make allegory obsolete.

The big question here is — up in the sky where the big questions can be pondered — is Coetzee saying that for white South Africans there is no meaningful or moral survival without apartheid? Is he saying that apartheid is as much social system as physical body; is he saying that whites are irredeemable?

I'm about to fall into one of those disturbed sleeps one falls into on airplanes. Now it is amplified by Coetzee's dread. In the gaps of waking and sleeping, I plummet into the middle of *Paradise*. There, there is an exquisite chapter called "Divine." It opens at a wedding with a sermon on love which you are drawn into like being drawn stunningly into hell, well, into clarity. "God is not interested in you," declares the preacher. Here Morrison suggests that life in the Diaspora can't be put right, the imagination cannot suffice — not on love, not on grace, not on exile. Not on any thing that she can imagine at this moment anyway. The bride is a girl with a torn heart.

Why do I find this chapter "exquisite" then? Is it my own sense of hopelessness and doom? Does Morrison confirm my dread? Is dread the equivalent of beauty in the Diaspora? Is Coetzee's dread of another kind?

You have a lot of time to think, going to Australia. There is a portion of the journey where you feel that you will never see land again. Most people on the plane are sleeping through this part. I am worried about *Disgrace*. If Coetzee's white professor is irredeemable, his Blacks are horribly so. Coetzee's Blacks are acquisitive, predatory, rapine, and brutal. They have the unfortunate opacity of all Blacks in the imagination of a racially constructed whiteness — they are, in a word, scary. There is the growing or overbrooding presence of avenging Blacks. First is Petrus, a hard-working but acquisitive man. So acquisitive that Lurie's daughter is also game. But there are more scary Blacks to come — three of them — one of them a boy who is connected to Petrus by family and perhaps all of them related to Petrus by plot. Lurie and Lucy first meet them on foot along the road. Then follows the brutal rape of Lucy and the beating and burning of Lurie. As mysteriously as they arrive, they disappear. They are ubiquitous. Rape is universal but the trope of the Black rapist is an overwhelming one. It is also predictable and over-used. I was startled by its deployment in *Disgrace*.

Below me, out there in a vast darkness, or is it light yet, the international dateline is turning yesterday into tomorrow. Changing everything, even moments. So simply. In *Paradise*, without physical description of the women at the convent, Morrison leaves us to disentangle our own racial codes with the smallest of signifiers, that line: "They kill the white girl first." Reviewers have gone in pursuit and disagree on just who that is in the text. Odd the discomfort that this brings. And here I remember Coetzee and a similar discomfort. But is it? He says in his earlier work, race doesn't exist. She says in *Paradise*, race exists in the collective mind — but it doesn't exist really, does it? We all obviously find it important — we handle it, we leave it glaringly untouched, we circum-vent it . . . like the world, in this airplane's clumsy flight.

In *Disgrace*, the Black rapists are spectres of white fear and Lurie, is like Kurtz in *Heart of Darkness*, "reduced" (by savagery, it is intimated) to savagery. Race exposes allegory. Allegory cannot lift race in its universal wings. Does Coetzee see it, I wonder, as I drift off again, for in the "universal" the "black rapist" trope *is* universal. Lucy says, "I think they are rapists first and foremost. Stealing things is just incidental. A sideline. I think they *do* rape." (not my italics). The power of this trope is absolutely fascinating to me. How it eradicates, here in Coetzee's text, a century of brutal injustice; how its possibility comes to justify, intentionally or not, "keeping the blacks down."

Well, all this stems from having to discern whether one is being asked to dance or whether one is being ordered to conjugate a verb in another language. It is not the job of writers to lift our spirits. Books simply do what they do. They sometimes confirm the capricious drama of a childhood living room. When you think that you are in the grace of a dance you come upon something hard. In *Paradise*, Blacks can never live peacefully because of racism. In *Disgrace*, whites can never live peacefully without racism. Perhaps myth and allegory are worn out, perhaps they fail as imaginative devices. But so too reality. Sydney is ahead of me and behind me are hours of vertigo and restless sleep which I've left in two books.

## Maps

> Every shadow made by an opaque body smaller than
> the source of light casts derivative shadows tinged by
> the colour of the original shadows.
>
> From Leonardo da Vinci's notes
> on light and shadow, circa 1492

## Up Here

Calibishie. Up here you are in the world. It is ochre and blue-
black and nothing you can call rock but if you can imagine
before rock, molten obelisk, walls of volcanic mud jagging
out into the ocean, and the ocean, voluminous, swift and
chaotic. But perhaps it is we who are chaotic and the ocean
orderly, we in disarray and the orange ochre rock mannered.
Up here you are in the world and you want to stay, though
in the evening your eyes reach over the windward mist to
Marie-Galante in the horizon closing down, and in Marie-
Galante you conjure the chaos you know of a city.

Perhaps over on Marie-Galante someone else, like you, looking south to Dominica, Calibishie where you are, someone
else sitting on a similar veranda, someone else is conjuring

chaos. Though they cannot see a city in Calibishie, so their eyes would brush past farther on to Marigot.

So you are here alone then, and you cannot hold on or control the orderliness of the real world, but you are here as all around you the light goes suddenly and quickly as light goes here and the noises of dusk rise, describable and indescribable; the noise of crickets singing loudly and all at once, beginning at the same moment as darkness envelops you. Up here in Calibishie you are in the world and wondering what is the sound you make, what is the business you do, who are you in this orderliness that does not seem to need you. Well, you sit there on a veranda at Calibishie and you feel everything, feel the soft moist breeze across your body, smell the musk of the sea, hear the creak and shush of the poinciana. As suddenly and as quietly your eyes shift from conjuring a city to save you. Suddenly and as quietly everything is passing, all you've lived, and you are sitting in the lap of something big, some intimacy.

The next day we drive up into the Carib territory and it is about midday and only fools like us are out on the road in the middle of the day when bare feet burn on the asphalt and the rain forest road is humid and long. You get the sense that the mountain road and the tree fern and the palmiste have been here absorbing and deflating other foolish incursions.

The maxi taxi stops and we get out, going into the shop. A Carib man looks me in the eye as if he knows me and I settle into his look and I buy a hat whose strands of flex, he explains, have been buried in levels of mud, dyed there in grades of brown and red. We climb back into the van and he looks at me again as if I should be staying and where am I off to now, and I am half surprised but half convinced that, well, of course I should be staying. He sent his son, like my brother, to give me a small basket as a gift, as if to say, "Well, here then, go if you're determined, but take this with you." I had noticed at the back of the shop, my sister, his daughter, a whole world was in her face, 3000 years of Ciboney, then Arawak, then Carib canoeing north from South America, before it was South America, 1000 AD. In her face all the battles against the French and English for two centuries, the hit and hit and run and the intractable mountains that kept this island Carib until 1763; until settling to the west and east they crept into her face, too. In her face, now African, which people? Ga? Ashanti? Ibo? Washed in, wept in, with all the waters of the hundreds of rivers and rivulets. I swam some of those rivers — sluggish Cribiche, the crackling fresh Sarisari, the swelling magnificent Layou, the river Claire, the river Crapaud, Taberi, Mulaitre, Ouayaperi — I tried to swim them all, all 365, and say them all over and over — River Jack, Rivière Blanche, Canari, River Douce, Malabuka, Perdu Temps. And all this

Dahomey in her face that would name the valley to the southwest the Valley of Desolation.

Well I left them in the road of the Carib territory, waving, and the van moved on, chewing up still-rugged highway over to Mahaut and Massacre. "Massacre," Rochester says in Jean Rhys' *Wide Sargasso Sea*, "And who was massacred here? Slaves?" "Oh no," Antoinette answers, foreshadowing her own erasure in Charlotte Brontë's *Jane Eyre*, "Not slaves. Something must have happened a long time ago. Nobody remembers now." When Rochester arrived in Massacre it was raining, ". . . huge drops sounded like hail on the leaves of the tree, and the sea crept stealthily forwards and backwards." He had feared that it might be the end of the world. When I arrived in Massacre it was gleaming, the sky a glittering blue and the road, which was sea and road at once, was full of people. The rum shop was busy and someone in the van said, "These Massacre people are always on the street, day or night. This town is always lit up." The town had a certain feeling of careening, all bare feet and flowered dresses, all old men with sticks and young ones with soccer balls, all hips held to laugh and children playing fiercely. Rhys would have longed for it even more than she longed for it in *Voyage in the Dark*.

The next morning I wake up in Roseau, the sunlight pouring through the jalousie and something else, the sound of Roseau, nothing sweeter than children going to school, sun burning their lips in laughter and their own schemes, nothing sweeter in the morning than Roseau women singing in patois, "Ça qa fait na?" and answering, "Moi la!" How are you? I'm there! I'm there. I've lain in rooms in cities listening before, but this Roseau is the sweetest sounding. You can't tell the difference between laughing and quarrelling. So I'm there and I wait until the morning sound turns to mid-morning and then the silence of noon and then it starts all over again and then, like and unlike Calibishie, because Roseau is a city, night's intimacy passes over the buildings and streets and commerce and over the water again.

## Maps

> Every light which falls on opaque bodies between equal angles produces the first degree of brightness and that will be darker which receives it by less equal angles, and the light and shade both function by pyramids.
>
> From Leonardo da Vinci's notes
> on light and shadow, circa 1492

## Armour

I am always in the armour of my car in these small northern Ontario towns. They are unremittingly the same. There is a supermarket, a liquor store, a video store where there is also milk, bubble gum, and Coca-Cola, and inevitably a pickup truck parked in a lot. There is sometimes a garage with a greasy man or two and a harassed guard dog or an old dog suffering from hip dysplasia. The small town to which I drive every morning and which I never become so familiar with as not to think of my car as my armour, my town is the same as the rest. And yes, there is also a cemetery and a church, two churches for a population that can hardly divide into two. The garage in this town has a mechanic who hates to talk. He keeps a dog tied up on a filthy mattress inside the garage. One day I see this dog who has also been cultivated for fierceness and I want to let him go, even if he will bite me. The mechanic who is also the gas attendant is a middle-aged man. He has been burned by wind and snow and gas fumes. His face is scaled red with white patches. His mouth is a tight thin wire. His jeans have grown small, but he hasn't disowned them. Sometimes I am not sure if he will sell me gas. Sometimes I am not sure if the corner store will rent me a video. Money is not always the currency here. Nor books, which I could offer. There might be no way of exchanging even the things that strangers might exchange. Here I feel that I do not share the same consciousness. There is some other rhythm these people grew up in, speech and gait and probably sensibility.

There are ways of constructing the world — that is, of putting it together each morning, what it should look like piece by piece — and I don't feel that I share this with the people in my small town. Each morning I think we wake up and open our eyes and set the particles of forms together — we make solidity with our eyes and with the matter in our brains. How a room looks, how a leg looks, how a clock looks. How a thread, how a speck of sand. We collect each molecule, summing them up into flesh or leaf or water or air. Before that everything is liquid, ubiquitous and mute. We accumulate information over our lives which bring various things into solidity, into view. What I am afraid of is that waking up in another room, minutes away by car, the mechanic walks up and takes my face for a target, my arm for something to bite, my car for a bear. He cannot see me when I come into the gas station; he sees something else and he might say, "No gas," or he might simply grunt and leave me there. As if I do not exist, as if I am not at the gas station at all. Or as if something he cannot understand has arrived — as if something he despises has arrived. A thing he does not recognize. Some days when I go to the gas station, I have not put him together either. His face is a mobile mass, I cannot make out his eyes, his hair is straw, dried grass stumbling toward me. Out the window now behind him the scrub pine on the other side of the road, leaves gone, or what I call leaves, the sun white against a wash of grey sky, he is streaking toward me like a cloud. Frayed with air. The cloud of him arrives, hovers at the window. I read his face coming apart with something — a word I think. I ask for gas; I cannot know what his response is. I pass money out the window. I assume we have got the gist of each other and I drive away from the constant uncertainty of encounters. I drive through the possibility of losing solidity at any moment.

## Maps

The early Romans drew maps based solely on itineraries, not attesting to science or geographic study. Simply maps of where they were going. So that a map looked like a graph of horizontal lines of roads heading to a destination.

## Pinery Road and Concession 11

The water pump chortles and the car stops abruptly. I am in a great field of snow at Pinery Road and Concession 11. In the summer here the trees form a cathedral over the road. Today they are frostbitten, their summer communion broken, their branches brittle.

The car stops. I try several times to turn the engine over, but nothing. It is three kilometres back to town where there is a post office at which perhaps the librarian who is also the post mistress might allow me to use the phone. I have been living out here in the bush for two years now. This place fills me with a sense of dread but also mystery. I fear the people more than the elements, which are themselves brutal. Winters here are harsh and long. I spend mornings getting the house warm. The house is still six kilometres away from Pinery Road and Concession 11 where my car has stalled.

I have inherited this fear of people from my grandmother. She never went outside the house except on the rare occasion when some bureaucratic necessity, some official order, warranted it. She was a fearful woman, a private woman. To ask a neighbour for anything, which straightened circumstances necessitated, caused my grandmother much anxiety and shame. She would have the family wait until the last possible resistance gave way before sending a carefully worded message to a neighbour for help. I am the same way. I sit and panic and wait and wait until the last moment before calling for mercy. Then I compose my plea, then I agonize about the composition — is it too brief, is it too long, is it overweening, is it too dignified to warrant sympathy? When I am sure, deciding most times on brevity, I approach the telephone three or four times. Sometimes this last process takes a whole day, sometimes two. I wait again to see if I cannot do without what I need. Does it really matter? Can I not find it another way? Is asking for help really the only thing I can do?

So I sit in the car at Pinery Road and Concession 11 wondering how I can get the car to move without going for help. Help exposes you to people's disdain was how my grandmother saw it. In this way my grandmother assumed nothing of anyone, nothing good, perhaps; she only assumed her own acts. What will the librarian say when I walk into town and ask her for the favour of using the phone? What foolish act of mine caused me to have to ask? I contemplate leaving the car there in the middle of the road and walking deliberately into the snow and the forest.

All around me is forest, except to one side there is an open field where cows graze in the summer. There are few houses along the three kilometres to my house — lone buildings on acres of forbidding forest. In the winter they are for the most part empty. Like my grandmother, for me the outside is treacherous. This is country where people mind their own business; they are as cold and forbidding as the landscape. They live out here free of the city, they guard what they call their "property," they eschew city life, they love country music's lonesome and outlaw tenors. They are suspicious of strangers. I can only imagine nightmarishly what they think of me. I am grateful for their sense of privacy.

When you live out here, six kilometres from Pinery Road and Concession 11, you become impervious to the cold. The winter is thermal. You go out on your "property" only in jeans and a flannel shirt. Granted, your feet must be well shod for the wetness, but you gradually do not need a jacket. You need a dog and you need a gun, but not a jacket or a coat. I have left the dog at home. Unfortunately I do not have a gun or perhaps walking the six kilometres home could be easy.

Snow is quiet. It is not like rain. It has the sound of nothing happening. It is like a deep breath held and held. I sit in the car and the cold of it begins to creep in. There is a way that land defeats you, just the sum of it. In a cold car at Pinery Road and Concession 11, you notice its width.

When it's covered in snow you know that it is hardly sleeping. It is like a huge brown-backed being waiting.

In the snow every distance is long. At Pinery Road and Concession 11 there is a peace, except it is too much peace. I imagine remaining in the car until all this peace and snow covers me and I melt into the forest. I settle into eternity. I would prefer the world to stop now, or at least my part in the world at Pinery Road and Concession 11. But it doesn't, so I contemplate the walk to Burnt River.

Burnt River is where the librarian doubles as the post mistress. I cannot say how I have managed to live in this country place. Summers and winters. Like my grandmother I hardly speak to anyone. I keep to myself. Each morning when I am not sitting in my dead car at Pinery Road and Concession 11, I go to town, Kinmount, about ten minutes by car along Highway 121. I buy a newspaper, bubble gum from the gum machine, and on occasion any supplies I need for the house, my bunker on Concession 11. Gradually, but it has taken me months, I exchange a few words with Mr. Dettman at Dettman's Store, where I buy my newspaper and bubble gum. Dettman's also rents videos. It would not be too much of an exaggeration to say that I've seen every video Dettman's has in stock. Mr. Dettman, no more talkative than I, manages something approximating civility when I enter. A nod. I nod back but I am much more eager to please or not to cause offence here in this town, which is all white except for the Chinese people who took over the restaurant in my last year in the bush. So I not only nod but also say good morning and take some time looking over the movies for anything new. Nothing, so I buy my paper, my bubble gum, and on the mornings when I feel that I must show Mr. Dettman a loyalty, a bottle of distilled water. Then I get into my car and head to Concession 11. I enjoy my bubble gum on the way home. Sometimes I buy two pieces. I like to put my quarter in the machine and wait for the routine surprise of colour. I like the reds and the blues. I never buy more than two pieces or else there would be no reason to go to town except the newspaper.

If the red flag on my mailbox is up I am delighted. It means that there is news from away. My grandmother's "away" was England. Mine is Toronto or Ottawa, sometimes England or the United States. To be sure, one of the benefits of living in the bush is that it gives you distance. A lovely distance from everything. There is no urgency, as when you live in a city. It does not matter if you do not return a phone call or get some very important thing done. Very important things do not need to get done. Very important things do not happen. Except for the porcupine climbing the pine in spring, or the moose crossing the river one winter, or the snowplow plowing me into the driveway after all my shovelling. Or the wood I have to fetch and pile near the stove to be dried and the other pile I have on the veranda. All right, all the stages of wood I have to arrange, the pile under the tarp I have to shake the ice off of, the pile near the doorway. The whole business of ordering the wood in the fall from the farmer who does not have a phone. Sound man. I drive to his place down Highway 503 and call to him. He comes out up to his arms in blood. I hope that he hasn't killed his wife, but I am already out of my car and cannot retreat. She appears a few seconds later to put my mind at rest. Calfing he says, explaining his hands. I order two cords of wood; I give the money to his wife and leave. When he brings the wood several days later his arms are blistered. Poison ivy, he says. He drops the wood in the driveway, and we talk about wood: how much I'll need; when the cold seems like it's going to come; no, I might not burn any wood till late October this year counting by the *Farmers' Almanac*; oh yes, this will do me fine this year, not like last year when I ran out.

These are the very important things of living in the country. There is a drought each year in midsummer. The river up the road recedes; my well water is not even two feet high. In May, June, and July you can hardly go outside for the mosquitoes and black flies. I have a green cylindrical hat with netting for walking; I have a white mosquito net draped around my bed. I bought it second-hand somewhere. There were a few holes in it I had to mend. It's very good laying under it, making sure no mosquitoes get in when I do. I lie there at night in the very, very dark of the country, the smell of pine and cedar around me, the very quiet of the bush pressing in, and I listen until I fall asleep.

But now I am sitting in the car at Pinery Road and Concession 11 deciding to make my way to Burnt River and the post mistress. It is mid-afternoon. I've left the dog at home alone all morning. She'll be needing to get out by now. She's a good dog. Aggressive and unfriendly. I get out and lock the car. There's really no need here, even if it wasn't stalled. There is no one here who would steal it. This is not a desperate place. It is a still place. To steal a car requires a kind of quick desperation. If there is desperation here it is the kind that is slow burning, the kind that drinks beer and smokes cigarettes and is overwhelmed by the bush or the river, the kind that makes the body grow large and lumbering and listless. There is no one on this road today. Only me. I stand in the middle of the road and take in my choices: to the left along Pinery Road where I've never turned; to the right six kilometres of turns and bends and possible surprises to my house and the dog; to the north into the bush of deep snow or to the north-west into the open field where I can lie down and be swallowed up by tonight's snowfall and wind; or to the post office. Cautious, I head for the post office.

What I am doing out here I do not know. I mean of course in the sense that I did not know I would end up here. *End up* is not the right phrase. My life is not over. *Land* may be a better word. Landing is what people in the Diaspora do. Landing at ports, dockings, bridgings, stocks, borders, outposts. Burnt River is another outpost, another destination. Conrad was a seaman who had his darkness; I have Burnt River. But I had no destination in mind. I am without destination; that is one of the inherited traits of the Diaspora. I am simply where I am; the next thought leads me to the next place. I have come to Burnt River to write. I have ended up writing a few books in Burnt River. I landed in Burnt River and I am writing a few books. I had no money so I came to Burnt River. I left somewhere else and came to Burnt River. I am in Burnt River. I am lucky that the name of this place is beautiful, though it is beautiful in that same oppositional way as everything else. River and Burnt. The history of this name I do not know, but it is like all names in the New World cut through with something terrible that happened. Altered, as River is by Burnt. And what this place was called in its own language I do not know. But River must have been in it. One night, one of the rare nights that friends visited, sleeping in the upstairs of my house someone had a dream of something with a great wing passing over the house. The next morning one of those friends who was Six Nations asked, "Whose land is this, I wonder?" Whoever's it was, they had passed over the house. I thought of this winged being when I was alone. Sometimes at night I felt it pass and linger at the tops of the scrub pines. It was not a peaceful thing, though it meant no harm to me, I think.

You would not know it to look at me but I am like my grandmother a person of sure perimeters. Though I have arrived all the way here in Burnt River I am not adventuresome. Burnt River is just below the forty-fifth parallel, and I have arrived here — well, to be sure I have meandered here — from the tenth parallel. But that is not to say much. I still take the small steps of my grandmother; I lift my eyes only to the immediate area of the house I live in, the small bit of road I can see from the window. Though I look intently and I know each dead weep of grass within my view. I pore over the spindly shrub pine clacking together in the wind. One winter I shovelled the hundred-foot driveway, three feet deep in snow, the whole winter long, crying at my misfortune, before I got the idea to call a snowplow. I always had the idea that while my grandmother did not move much she observed well. So, hunkered in my house in Burnt River I scrutinize each window's drama of trees and sky. But in the beginning I did not notice wildflowers. So intent on the hardship of living out here and missing the city and missing friends. I never bathed in the river, I never jumped off the bridge in town. Life was always something waiting to happen later. Until one day at this same spot at Pinery Road and Concession 11, when it was fall and all the grass had turned brown and wilted, I saw something violet. I thought, "What a fool!" struggling up like that with winter coming. And all through the fall I thought, "Well, I never!" when violet kept appearing on the side of the road. Finally I thought, "Well, what else is possible? Nothing but to make a go of it, I suppose."

After a hundred metres or so, I turn and look back at the car. Its hulk is already embraced by the snowy road. The road knows that wherever you find yourself you are.

## More Maps

According to my grandmother, the world was the house, its perimeter its shadow which the sun made each morning to the back of the house, withdrew at midday, and refigured in the afternoon in the front yard. Her bed was the ship of the world and her broom was her harpoon to spear us when we reached beyond its boundaries. She sailed in that bed, sending signals to the grocery store, written on brown paper bags. One pound red beans, ten pounds rice, five pounds sugar, two pounds salt fish, four pounds split peas, ten cents worth of oil, one-half pound lard; on copy book leaves in her rickety writing she ordered the shopkeeper, "Dear Lloyd, please trust me these goods, until . . ."

She sent children in directions she herself never arrived at. To Cipero Street, Rushworth Avenue, High Street, Carib Street, Coffee Street to Harris Promenade; Cipero Street and Coffee Street. Places whose names carried the last whiff of receded cane estates; Carib Street, curling up a shattered mountain, and High Street, rising from a wharf. Harris Promenade where she once fainted and where eighteenth-century Spaniards once promenaded in the evening. There was a bandstand there, palm trees painted white, a Catholic church, an Anglican church, a courthouse. She sent us to towns called Cocoyea Village, Marabella, Vista Bella, Les Effort, Princess Town, Mayaro. She only navigated and travelled the seven windows of the house, and the two doorways.

*October*

1

Marlene and I are sitting in a café on the Danforth. She has
been ill recently. I haven't seen her in a while. I have been
afraid that she would succumb to her illness. I cannot bear
the possibility of losing her. So I haven't seen her. An odd
way of loving her, I know. It's the way I love my family. If I
don't see them, if I don't know the particular details of their
lives, I won't miss them when they go, or I'll stave off their
leaving, or they cannot possibly leave without my knowing.
If I do not know a thing then it has not happened.

Last summer, I decided that I must see her, because along
with this kind of reasoning come sudden attacks of panic as
to the logic of it, sudden misgivings as to the inherent miscal-
culations, the smaller, incremental losses — the minutes I can
still see her with my eyes passing, the conversations I am pre-
empting. I have been fearful lately, which is not to say
anything really. I have been living in Burnt River alone with
my dog for the past three years. One can easily grow paranoid
in the silent snow and the lightless dark, the big nights and
the short grey days. It seems that it is always winter here. I
long for the summers, when I am pursued by the sun around
the veranda and look for Blue Jays and foxes and try to cate-

gorize the seemingly infinite variations of pine. I know tama-
rack grows near water and bears will visit if there is a drought.
I am as watchful in the summer, of the road, of the well, of
movement in the river, of cars that seem to slow down at my
driveway. But Burnt River, summer or winter, is not sufficient
to explain my present fear. My fear has a particular origin.

It began in another house on a cliff falling into a road.
Marlene lived in that house. In the back of the house there
was an office where she and I worked. From the back of the
house you could see the Carenage, St. George's Harbour,
and out to the Caribbean Sea. Above this house, one
Tuesday morning, Marlene and I along with three others
heard bombers in the sky. It was around 5 a.m. The noise
woke us up. We switched the radio on only to hear that the
Americans had invaded the island, Grenada. The radio
played patriotic songs rousing the people and the military
to report to various places — St. Patricks, Sauteers . . . Then
it abruptly went off the air. I showered quickly, thinking
somehow that if I showered and put on my jeans and sneak-
ers I would be ready for this invasion. Everyone else in the
house awoke and did the same. In the dawn, from the
balcony, we could see warships out in the ocean. We were
trapped in this house for several days. We did not know
what was going to happen to us. I thought that we were
going to die. We paced, we drank rum, we talked about the

falling revolution, we quaked and crouched in a corridor when the bombs fell, we waited listening for the burst of the bombing raids. I felt myself growing thinner and thinner with nervousness.

Marlene and I are sitting now in a café on the Danforth. It is fifteen years later. There is a question I need to ask her. I have finally figured out this question and I am finally not ashamed or embarrassed to ask her. I haven't seen her in a long time. She is ill, her left shoulder is slightly immobile. We are drinking cappuccinos and I ask her, "Marlene, did we, ah, did you go crazy after? Did you have trouble with life?"

## 2

It is the 19th of October 1999 and I remember this. I was in Grenada; there was a coup on the 19th of October. A state of emergency. Four days later the Americans invaded the island. On the day of the coup I was sleeping late. I had been ill. I would usually be at work by 9 a.m. I would walk along Harris Street to the office. Harris Street was three or four tiers up the hill surrounding the harbour. I would see the ocean to my left. I would see schoolchildren on my way. They would look combed and shine. They would idle along their way to school. I would see middle-class women cutting flowers and trimming bougainvillea fences. I would notice other people going to work. Every now and again, I would slip on the gravelled road, I would see the houses of St. George's in steep ascending stacks around the harbour.

On the 19th of October that year, I slept late. I lived in a house with a breadfruit tree in the front yard. The house was blue. The house was on a typical hill. Hills were inevitable in St. George's. The whole town inclines from a harbour. The incline is steep and murderous anywhere. In the rainy season a deluge would gouge the brown earth from the front of the house to the back. The breadfruit would fall, bashing themselves on the concrete steps. Once I saw a mongoose in the backyard. My house was made of concrete and painted blue. Next door there was a young woman with a baby and a little boy in a flimsy wood house. Her front door was rotted away at the bottom. She had white frayed curtains which swung haphazardly in the window to my side. That day I didn't hear the baby crying. I usually heard the baby crying in the morning. But my head was full of a pain and fever, so I didn't hear the baby cry. I was awakened instead by the sound of a great crowd. This same burning head had led me to this island. I had come here in search of a thought, how to be human, how to live without histori-cal pain. It seemed to me then that a revolution would do it. But I woke up that morning not because I heard the baby's usual noise but because I heard the crowd.

Three days before, the prime minister had been placed under house arrest because it was alleged he had violated democratic centralism. In a moment of naïveté, of textbook fascination, I had supported this decision. The same moment of naïveté of his jailers, no doubt, but I thankfully was not in charge of a whole country, though it was me, or people like me, who had never held power and who had only had dreams and who when touched by the reality of it could not hold it, people who, although they spoke about the imperialist power of the United States, did not some-how believe that power. Or perhaps they were people so consumed by the intimate nature of their disagreements that they could not sense that anyone else could be concerned with their trouble nor that there were outside forces about to put an end to their project. This part of the story is history. The coup took place, the Americans invaded. That was the end of the socialist path in Grenada and the English-speaking Caribbean. And so far stories end like this in history books. Whatever the textbook analyses, though, whatever the representations of tinpotism from abroad, whichever pundits said in clear hindsight that they knew it was coming, all of that was irrelevant that morning. That morning felt as close as family, as divine as origins.

I think it was a Friday. As I said, I woke up ill. A headache blinding me like the sun across my eyes. And the sound of a great crowd in the morning. Not the baby. The baby's mother had already taken the baby to meet the crowd. The crowd was on top of another hill above me. Someone ran to my door and said, "They free Maurice!" It was a friend. She said that she was leaving now, going back to the country because there would be trouble in town. Said goodbye to me as if she would never see me again. She left. We never saw each other again. I dressed anxiously. The fever in my head felt as if I had inhaled water. I quickly summoned my resources to leave the house. There was now a strange quiet, stranger than the usual quiet of mid-morning there. This quiet was an empty quiet, as if I were the only one left on the street. I hurried along Harris Street trying to find someone to talk to. A few people were still at home but turned away when I passed by. They did not want to speak to anyone, least of all someone who had lived among them only a few months. The sea to my left was its usual blue, the slight wind from the ocean at its usual play, the sun now smart and piercing, my head feeling as if I were drowning in air. No one was at the office when I arrived. I waited until Alice got there and the new clerk we had hired, a young woman from Cariacou. Alice bustled in saying that she had just come in a taxi and that she was going to return home because there was going to be trouble. She seemed to know that all was falling down. She gave me a note for Marlene, something about her paycheque and where to send it. She cleaned out her desk, putting the contents into her large black purse. I asked her if she wasn't going to town to see what was happening. She said, "No, my dear, I'm going home." The woman from Cariacou looked as if she wanted to bolt. She had only started work that month. Alice told her to go home. Things passed over her face. She had just got a good job, was this the end of it? Nothing like this ever happened in Cariacou; she ought to run, go back home. She had to go to town to fetch the transport to the place where she now lived in Goauve. I said I would go with her, go to town myself and see what was going on. We locked up and Alice left, heading out of the way of the trouble. The woman from Cariacou and I walked around the incline of the harbour and down toward Market Square.

Marlene had not been at the office, nor at home on the other side of the building. I suspected that she might have been in town and that I would find her there. The woman from Cariacou and I got to Market Square. She had planned to go to the taxi stand at the centre of the square and seek transport to Gouave but it looked impossible. The streets running to it and Market Square itself were teeming with people. They had freed Maurice from house arrest and borne him down to the square and up to the fort. My head still ached but the sun had somehow squeezed the fever out of me, or perhaps it had risen beyond my being able to understand that I was ill. I was stunned, everything was out of control, there were thousands and thousands of people milling around, throngs were heading toward the fort, up the steep incline. I saw a man on the upper balcony of a store waving a flag and chanting in exhaustion that Maurice was free and that those who had arrested him should be killed. He was stripped and hoarse from screaming. His eyes met mine for a moment. I recognized him as one of the cadres in the party. I thought that he looked nervous for that moment. The thought ran across my mind that he was an outside provocateur, not really on any side here, perhaps an American agent. I passed into the crowd below him and headed with the woman from Cariacou toward the fort. I heard his hoarse voice trailing off. The atmosphere was ripe with possibilities.

I cannot say how I felt that day except that everything, every minute, was a surprise. I was sure of nothing, though I was hopeful throughout. The way children who know nothing are hopeful always, unable to judge what the next moment will bring. And I gave up all thoughts, all of my movements, to this hope. So I walked up to the fort. I was inside and outside of whatever was going on and so I observed the provocateur on the balcony at the same time that I took my hopes with me up to the fort like everyone else. I moved not with any deliberateness or purpose or foresight. I was less determined than the crowds of people.

The fort hill was an area smaller than half a soccer field. There were, as I recall, two or three buildings there, an army barrack, a main building, and some other structure. I cannot say that for certain. That morning was a daze with my fever and the masses of people and the air so full, so full of danger and expectation. The buildings were a blur. But I saw everyone who would die later that day. I remember them. Jackie was in yellow, she had a cigarette in her hand, she was fiery, waving the cigarette about and talking decisively; Vincent was next to her, I think his jersey was blue, he was punching the air with his hands as he spoke; Maurice was inside the darkened doorway. Reaching the top of the fort hill, the woman from Cariacou and I found a spot on the cliffside. The cliff dropped through jagged rocks into a road. We stood there waiting for Maurice to speak. The crowd was celebratory. I recall smiling, laughing with the woman from Cariacou.

It is possible to laugh in moments which turn out to be terrifying and tragic. You do not know that it is going to be so, you are living in the present, in each second, and so there was laughter in the crowd. Something good had happened: Maurice had been freed and the tension of the last three days had ended in celebration. We were joking and laughing, thinking that all was put to right again and perhaps we would walk down from this hill, drink a rum and Coke, and go to sleep again. You do not know that someone who is wearing yellow and smoking a cigarette and someone who is dressed perhaps in blue and is a man of laughter and someone else standing in a doorway not six feet away from you will be killed one hour from now. The three people you are looking at are three strides away from you; you can call to them. They will be murdered in an hour; their bodies will be dragged behind this same fort and never recovered. Perhaps they will be dumped in the ocean or perhaps buried in a quarry; the yellow shirt and the blue shirt will be soaked in their blood. The shadow which is Maurice in the doorway will call to Jackie who is in yellow to come with him as they are dragged away. A soldier will call her a bitch; another will put the butt of his rifle in Maurice's face. You cannot know all this looking from your footing on the gravelled portion of the hill, then looking toward the building where they are still alive.

Two cars came up the hill, stopped, and a few men jumped out. They opened the trunk and took out four or five AK-47s. My friend, the woman from Cariacou, tugged at my arm and said, "Let's go!" Her face was stricken. I continued laughing. To soothe her I said to her, "Oh no, no, don't worry, it's over, nothing will happen. It's only guns." She tugged on my arm again, insistent, saying, "No, let's go now!" I don't know what made me listen to her. I hadn't known her that long. I just wanted to make her happy, to accompany her. I finally said all right, still laughing as if accommodating a child. We made our way through the crowd, I reluctantly, she pushing her way through quickly. I tried to slow her again, saying it was all right, that nothing more would happen. "Why would it?" I asked. She said, "You don't know." I didn't but I thought that I did. I thought that I knew more than she. The truth is I knew nothing at all that day. My head was in a fever, though my fever was forgotten by then, but even without it I did not know the thing that she knew, which she was trying to tell me. She could read the signs of her compatriots better than I. She knew where she lived. I lived like a poet lives, in a dream, in a wonderful dream which is always awakening to the hard things about life and then diving into the dream again for rescue. And that day I had a fever to compound it. But like a poet I left with her, just to console her. We walked down the hill and I said to her again, "Nothing else can happen. Look, if it does it's suicide, right? No, no, it's over." She said, "You wait and see." Market Square was still packed but more and more people were drifting toward the fort. She still could not find transport to Goauve. She decided to go to a friend's. We walked around Archibald Street. We parted near the fire station. I said I'd see her at work the next day if things were settled. It was the last time I saw her. I never thanked her for saving my life.

I thought about returning to the fort when I left the woman from Cariacou. As if I should go back now that I had seen her off, but then I thought that I should go to work to find Marlene and tell her what I had seen, so I went to the office. I had the keys, and the keys to Marlene's house. I climbed the steep hill from the fire station and up the track to the house. I went to the kitchen, got a glass of cold water from the refrigerator, and walked out onto the balcony which looked out to the fort. I saw the crowd there in the place where I was standing not five minutes ago. I raised the glass of water to my lips. I saw three armoured vehicles racing toward the fort. They were heavy, swift, and determined. Their motors were loud. I saw the top of them dip out of sight for a second at the fort road and then emerge on the hill. I heard the sound of gunfire. It was staccato but guttural. The crowd where I had been standing began running in all directions. I saw people leap from the cliff and bump raggedly down its side. There was nowhere to run. People threw their bodies down the cliff trying to get away. I could not hold the glass, the water spilling was like hard stones. I did not feel as if I was in my body. They looked like rags of cloth spilling over the cliff, tumbling. Some looked as if they expected to walk on air. The air dropped from my own body, there were a thousand bright stab wounds in my skin. Just then Marlene came in, breathless; she had been in Market Square. She had seen the armoured tanks go by her on the road. I tried to tell her about the cliff, people jumping off the cliff, I was just there, but I only recall pointing and the feeling that something had just passed close to my ear, softly buzzing.

We stood on the balcony, she and I, looking to the fort and the bodies collapsed on the cliff. I think I told her I was sorry about the glass that lay broken at our feet. More gunfire and then a flare went up in the sky. A white light which was almost imperceptible if not for the smoke trailing after it and the hard *voop* sound it made. It was a signal that someone was dragging Maurice and Jackie and Vincent to their deaths at that moment. What happens if you stand in a moment like this? Your own body must die, too, I suppose. Even if you do not know. Aren't we all implicated in each other? In any moment like this we must die, too. I was that body draping the cliff. I left myself on the cliff and I stood on the balcony with Marlene spilling a glass of water forever.

The curfew began. We were allowed to get food in the daytime until 6 p.m. Then we had to stay inside. The streets were quiet. Not even a dog walked by. The radio warned us about violating the curfew. When we did get out there were lines at the supermarket and more silence. Everyone looked as if they were alone, as if they did not know the person they lived with or the person who lived next door. We bought rum and sugar and rice and milk and split peas. We did everything in a stiff hurry, as if the day threatened to pass quicker than it usually did. As if the night was bearing down on us. At night the waiting for daylight again was interminable. The baby next door was quiet, as if he knew it was important to be still.

The thought that I should have died on the cliff covered me like a cloak. In my dreams I lay on the cliff, cut up, my limbs in disarray, the rocks breaking through, pebbles in my mouth. In my dreams I had stayed at the fort for five more minutes. I had convinced the woman from Cariacou to wait with me. We had been killed. When I awoke from these dreams I was not certain which was the dream and which was the real day.

It was a small place. Everyone knew everyone else. So everyone knew someone who had been killed. People listened to the radio with a personal pain, with thoughts of retaliation, with stony hearts or with a wound. The radio's attempts to sound distant and authoritative only rankled. The announcements themselves slipped into childish whinings of justifications for the killings. Once, I saw a fight between two brothers, grown men with the ability to kill each other. The fight was so physical, so fleshy, so reductive, as if abandoning any intellect, tearing their own skins off. These days reminded me of this. Finally it was personal.

The curfew lasted for three days and then there were battleships out in the ocean. Someone outside can never tell you how stupid war is, how insensible or how heartless. It is always much more so for you. You know full well because you are hopeless. Your body cracks to each sound of gunfire. You genuflect to each bombing attack of F15s. By the time it's over you are brittle, your teeth feel like crushed stones, you are skeletal, you have a single wire of electricity running up your back over which you have no control. That is only the corporeal. You had come here for some purpose. Small, certainly; foolish, certainly. It's still hard to say what it was now without someone sneering at it as if it is childish and impossible. I wanted to be free. I wanted to feel as if history was not destiny. I wanted some relief from the enclosure of the Door of No Return. That's all. But no, it had hit me in the chest and all the wind was gone out of me. It was all I could do to hold on to my mind, that is, to know the orderly passing of minutes and the idea that the sun comes up and it's daylight, it goes down and night comes. But of course nothing is the same. You climb into a car taking you to a U.S. army base on the island. You look at your hands and you look at your feet and you don't recognize them and you wait for what more is to be done to you. You find yourself at another base in another coming night waiting for an airplane to lift you out. But there is no you.

The fever I had on the first morning of the crisis seemed to last for years. As in a fever, you do not always know where you are. And then again, you know precisely and dreadfully where you are. A fever makes you acutely sensitive — to light, to shadow, to the unsubstantial, to chimera. You feel everything. Things happening miles away, things yet to happen at distances. Your ears hurt with sound.

Marlene and I are sitting now in a café on the Danforth. It is fifteen years later. She had since gone back and had been arrested by the Americans. Then she had gone to Africa to work again. This is a woman from whom I learned all I know. There is a question I need to ask her. It is hard to ask her. Perhaps she'll be disappointed in my lack of faith. But I have finally figured out this question and I am finally not ashamed or embarrassed to ask her. I haven't seen her in a long time. She is ill, her left shoulder is slightly immobile. We are drinking cappuccinos and I ask her, "Marlene, did we, did you go crazy after? Did you have trouble with life?"

"Yes," she says.

# Maps

*Îles cicatrices des eaux*
*Îles evidence de blessures*
*Îles miettes*
*Îles informes*
*Îles mauvais papier déchire sur les eaux*

Aimé Césaire, from *Cahier d'un Retour au Pays Natal*

## Soufrière, St. Lucia

A friend of mine told me a story. He is on a bus in Colombo.
The kind of bus you never find in the city where we live or
in any city in North America. The Colombo bus is packed,
literally, and speeding to its destination. My friend and
another man are hanging on to the pole at the open door.
The bus in fact does not have a door. The bus is so crowded
they are barely in the bus. My friend looks up the pole to
where it is held tenuously to the bus's ceiling. He sees a single
screw there holding the pole. He says to the man who he is
sharing the pole with as the bus flies through the city, "You
realize that our lives depend on that one little screw?" As if
my friend has intruded on him, the man says to him in exasperation, "So what!?" My friend cannot fathom this

response. He is angry with the man for pointing out the inevitability of death in our fragile existence. The man refuses his companionship and his grim camaraderie. So what.

One morning, walking the road by the jetty in Soufrière, leaving the market behind, its stalls scant on a weekday, the Pitons on the right, brown as dry season, the ocean white like the afternoon sun, I stop and say a chorus of Yemaya's song. I've walked here to do that, to bow down to the vast ocean and contemplate my smallness and its majesty and to simply acknowledge it by repeating a chorus I heard in a song by Celia Cruz. The ocean and the planet it weeps around, these are the only powers I truly respect. Over my shoulder is the steep hill to Anse Chastenet — women and men walk up the hill or catch a ride to their jobs in the opulent hotel cradled in its bay. I am at the jetty facing the small hill before Jalousie. This small hill is a severe contrast to the richness of Anse Chastenet. The shacks of the poor are crushed up against each other on this side. The town has levels of poverty. Poverty is not uncommon or remarkable anywhere on these islands. It is ordinary and there is an ebb and flow to it. There is an occasional easement from good luck or paydays or steady work or family in the country who send ground provisions or fish or wild meat. My own childhood was spent in one such town on another island in much the same way. Everyone around was relatively poor, poor being a kind of standard. But every now and then in such a town, such a country, there is a road like this one going to Jalousie — sometimes it is on a hillside facing a new highway, sometimes it is on the edge of a city — where the houses are crushed shacks of spare galvanized iron and reused wood and where the regular common privation is exaggerated and where, as if to be wicked, just in front of its face there is a casual opulence.

This morning, the sun not quite risen, I have awakened to go to the jetty to reason with Yemaya, the goddess of the ocean, to entreat her to help me with a certain problem — to make my life better, to send some worry away. I walk down to the jetty only three minutes away from the place I have rented. There is a hulk of an old ship there. There are boats tied up. I make my ablutions, dipping my hands into the water and signing to Yemaya. I am not religious, but this I do each time I am at the ocean. It is impossible for me not to be overwhelmed by it, not to pay respect. I never turn my back on it. I wet my forehead, throw handfuls of water into the air and back into the sea. Then I back away over the concrete breaker onto the asphalted roadway, praising Yemaya and asking for my favour. I complete my singing and I begin to walk toward Jalousie. The Pitons are to my right, those two wonderful mountains. Gros Piton and Petit Piton emerge from the ocean as if fresh every day. The mountains of which Walcott wrote, "Under the Pitons, the green/bay, dark as oil./Breasts of a woman, serenely rising."

There is a small hill past the market, past the jetty and the post office and the tourist board, and there to the left, the crushed shacks. The road edges into a cliff, a woman emerges from one of the shacks with a po covered by a piece of cardboard. She crosses the road toward the cliff, the ocean calm below. She flings the contents of the po over the side of the cliff, making sure that the po is empty, then crosses again to where she lives. Among these shacks, there is no running water, no electricity — no amenities. The woman is wearing a slip, her head is tied in white. She vanishes without noticing me. I continue up the hill and as I arrive at the place where she has emptied the po, there is the tremendous stench of human feces. The entire hillside cliff leading down to the ocean is covered in feces. The smell is overpowering and follows me as I try to escape it up the hill. My throat gags, my stomach heaves as I begin to run up the hill to get past the stench, trying to make my way to Jalousie. It is a long walk reaching Jalousie along the steep curve of the hill past villas and down into the bay. I come to the sea again and Yemaya. I do the same ablutions. I thank whoever her sister and brother gods are that it is not me on that hill in a slip and a head tie, but I cannot be so pitiless. I ask Yemaya why, what is it that we must live like that? She answers like a man hanging onto a pole in a bus in Colombo: "So what."

## Maps

The French took Gorée Island in the seventeenth century. It became a major station for slaving. On the upper floor of the "Maison des Esclaves" were quarters for the slave traders. The slaves were held in cells below. There were no amenities. The traders packed these cells to overcapacity. Chained and cramped in filth and excrement, many died from the inhuman conditions.

## Town

At the top of Soufrière in St. Vincent I meet three children. They are slender and inquisitive, as children here are. They are curious about everything and frank in their questioning. Though they have a shyness, a deference toward adults, once you address them they quickly come close as if you have been their friend for a long time. They are playing outside a school now closed for the evening. They are collecting tiny bits of chalk thrown out the window during the day by the teacher. They are two girls and a boy. Friends or brother and sisters, perhaps cousins.

Soufrière is a small village. It is a small village after a long drive from the capital. The road there is a road which leaves the capital, circles and climbs into the volcano. The volcano is called Soufrière. The earth is red and yellow. It is the dry season and every gust of wind raises dust. As we were driving to the top everyone on the road seemed covered in this reddish dust.

We arrive at the top, a baked village, houses along the road and some farther in on the sides of hills; some hidden in the recesses of the volcano. Near the school, I meet the children. One girl is playing the teacher, pointing to the boy, then the other girl, then her imaginary class for answers to her question. Anxious to deliver punishment for ignorance just like the real teacher. I see them and I walk toward them to talk. I used to be a child like this, fine boned and curious, playing school even when school was over. The boon of being the teacher was not to dispense knowledge but to dispense order and power. Mostly our game of school involved the teacher writing on the board some law of the classroom and the students whispering behind her back until they got caught, to wit the teacher would give strokes to the palm of the hand with a ruler. I walk toward them out of memory. They are talking away. Sometimes I look at children deep in discussion and I cannot remember what we spoke of as children. What talk did we fill all that time with? We rushed outside of houses, of classrooms, to be with each other and we chattered away at our own lives. So many hours we filled, but I cannot now remember how.

I am drawn across to where they are playing, to enter their childhood as if it were mine. To find there the warm simplicity of my own childhood, albeit interlaced with the dramas of hunger or violence or grief. Those recede as I see the children. Instead the childhood of play appears to me. There is a sureness in them which belies my own presence and what I have brought to this Soufrière with me. I have brought doubt. I have brought pity. I have brought a kind of condescension. I work for a development agency and I am here with others, including some local leftists, some progressive church people and some trade unionists, talking about development and underdevelopment. Our meeting is over and we decide to see Soufrière, to walk up to the volcano. There is a small village up here near the summit. The volcano last erupted in the 1980s, yet there is a small village here. There is this small village defying the earth, yellow and reddish, dry now. The volcano is silent now, sitting in the light mist it makes. This is not any place I know but I recognize the school and the children. One of the girls looks like someone I've been; someone I left behind long ago on another island, Trinidad. Happily.

I go over to the three playing at the side of the road near the school and I say hello. They answer tentatively. I have intruded and they are shy. They look at me with a mix of frankness and demur. I ask them what they are doing and they jump to explain since it is a question from an adult. Just playing . . . nothing . . . I stoop down beside them and take a piece of the chalk and begin to write my name on the asphalt. I say, "This is my name." They ask, "That is your name?" and they write their own. Before long we are friends. All three of them want to claim this stranger who has come up to Soufrière in the back of a truck and who comes over to talk to them. Before long I am asking them about school, about where they live. One of them looks at me and asks, "Miss, you from Town?"

From "Town." I am dumbfounded. I suddenly realize that I cannot answer this simplest of questions. I don't know where I'm from. I am from nowhere that I can explain to them. Town is their sense of the outside world. Town is the farthest that they can imagine. And I am from beyond Town. They have probably never been to Town but only heard of it as I had as a child. They have put me in a quandary. Where am I from? They seem sure that it must be Town, since Town is where everyone they do not know must be from. I feel like a child called on in the game of school but who doesn't know the answer to a simple question.

I arrived in Toronto before going to Town. Port-of-Spain, in my case. I had passed Town on my way to the airport without ever seeing it. Town. The word had summoned an old wonder. Town — one could get lost in it, one could be robbed, one could get into an accident, one could pick up with bad people, one could shop in high-class stores, one could be robbed. One would have to stay with Aunt Tina, who lived in Barataria, because Town was far. One would come home the next day with goods never seen before, with sweets never tasted before, with stories of how long the streets were, how busy, how one outsmarted a town person, how one got lost and found again, how hungry one was and how sick or how happy, how confident and how sophisticated one now was having been to Town. Town was nowhere that I was from. Town always frightened me. What if I was asked to go to Town by myself? I dreaded it. What if I could not find my way? What if I didn't look right? Would all the people in Town jeer at me? Would I end up crying on the corner of Frederick Street because I looked poor and could not find my way? Would I be taken away, kidnapped, by Mano Benjamin, the man who had kidnapped and tortured two girls, Dulcie and Lucy? But Town was a place one had to go eventually. It was a place one went to if one was lucky;

if one wanted to be anything but a country-boukie. I was not from Town. Town was a sophisticated place and in the face of that word, I was suddenly a plain girl who had never been to Town. So when the children asked me about Town with envy and wonder, I was speechless. Town used to be the furthest place in my imagination, too, the most horrific and the most glamorous. I had skirted Town a long time ago. I knew somehow that I had to avoid Town at all costs. I knew that I would never get to Town. I was afraid of Town. Town was like an axe waiting to fall. If I could get away, away, away, before having to go to Town, I would be thankful. It had been thirteen years since I'd left the country, but I had never been to Town.

When you travel everything goes with you, even the things you do not know. They travel; they take up space; they remain the things you do not know; they become the things you will never know. It had been a long time since I'd been from "there" and never ever had I been from Town. I had gone beyond Town. Town is a still-unexplored, still-unvisited, still-only-imagined place. Even now, decades later I am still afraid of Town. I am afraid that I would get lost there. It is bigger than any city I have been to: New York, or Boston, or Vancouver, or the city I live in, Toronto. I have navigated many cities — Amsterdam, London, Brussels, Paris — but Port-of-Spain is much more complicated. It is larger, impossible to navigate, ungraspable. It is still only a place in a calypso. I only know it because of newscasts on the radio many years ago: "In Port-of-Spain today crowds gathered . . ." I've only read about it in lines of poetry by Derek Walcott, lines like "The capitol has been repainted rose, the rails/ round Woodford Square the color of rusting blood." It is the most unknowable place in the world.

When the children asked me if I was from Town I became frightened. They were from some place. Here, where we stood. And they felt to me so assured, so certain, that they were from a place and I knew that I was not. I was from beyond Town. I could not describe where. I was therefore even out of my own reach. I envied them this assuredness. When I did not answer they looked at me with skepticism. I felt them lose interest in me. I recovered, saying, yes, I was from Town, and they began to pepper me with questions about Town which I could not answer. Then I said that I was from Town but I was living in America. "America!" they said, looking at me fabulously. "Yes, America," I said, having no word for Canada that was understandable. There was Here, there was Town, and there was America. That much I knew. Canada would have to be explained. It would be an awful mess and not as romantic. There was no sound of marvel like the sound that followed after "Town" or after "America." So I said, "Yes, America." That stopped them.

They lost interest in me anyway, because America was too big. I had overwhelmed them with America. Showing off. All to cover the fact that I was really from no place at all that I could describe. But I didn't really fool them; they were from someplace solid, this volcano, this hill, these people whom a volcano could not persuade to move. Their eyes took me in steadily. This was where they lived and I, I lived in the air.

The dusk was coming and they would have to go home. We would soon be leaving. A woman called a name from a house and the oldest girl turned, the one who had asked me if I was from Town. What a look she had. A look like being needed somewhere not for anything except to fill a familiar space on a lap, to receive a look of love, to be touched. She looked at the other two and said it was time to go home. I asked them where they lived and they pointed in a general way to the red earth out of which a zinc roof rose, a clothes-line and faint voices lifted on the intermittent breeze.

They ran off toward the place, waving at me, saying, "Miss, we have to go." Forgetting me.

*Maps*

My imagination was all rapture as I flew to the Register Office, and in this respect, like the apostle Peter, (whose deliverance from Prison was so sudden and extraordinary, that he thought he was in a vision) I could scarcely believe I was awake. Heavens! Who could do justice to my feelings at this moment! Not Conquering heroes themselves in the midst of a triumph — Not the tender mother who has just regained her long-lost infant, and press it to her heart — Not the weary, hungry mariner at the sight of the desired friendly port — Not the lover, when he once embraces his beloved mistress after she had been ravished from his arms! — All within my breast was tumult, wildness, and delirium!

Olaudah Equiano, on buying his freedom from slavery,
taken from *The Interesting Narrative of the Life of Olaudah
Equiano or Gustavus Vassa, the African.*
*Written by himself,* 1789

*Arriving at Desire*

It is only now I recall, when recalling is all art, that the first book I read and fell into like a fish falling into water was a book about the Haitian revolution of 1791. It was owned by my uncle, a teacher, and it had no cover. The pages were thick and absorbent, their colour a yellowish cream from age, the ink still dark and pungent. The book had lain in the bottom drawer of the wardrobe for as long as I could remember, with a book on mathematics — geometry — and a bible that was my grandmother's.

It was in the same drawer where my grandmother kept stores of rice and sugar, syrup shine breads, just-in-case goods, and, around Christmas, black cakes. She stored them under her good tablecloth, her good sheets, and the good pillowcases. So the book was walked over by little red sugar ants, it was bored through by weevils. It was mapped by silverfish. It was thick with the humidity of rainy season days and dry with the aridity of dry season days. It had no spine, though it had a back. It had no front cover. It had been sewn together, though the sewing was loose in some places, the thread almost rotted. It had been glued. The glue now caked off in caramel-like flakes from the original binding.

I recall the title running over the top of each page: *The Black Napoleon.* I recall that the first letter of each chapter was larger than the rest of the words. I remember certain names — Toussaint, Henri Christophe, Dessalines . . . I cannot recall the author. I've never checked to see if such a book actually existed. I've never looked for or found that particular book again. I prefer to think of it still at the bottom of the wardrobe drawer, waiting for me to fall into its face.

The wardrobe brown, the colour of mahogany. The bottom drawer was deep. It was heavy and it stuck at times, a pillowcase caught in the groove, wood lice altering its tracks, requiring some skill to open it quietly. There was always a fine dust in the base of the drawer, the work of colonies of insects moving their unseeable world to and fro. The book moved around from corner to corner, too. I do not remember if it began with the first chapter. I suspect not. The front cover had long disappeared.

What made me fall into this book was probably some raid on my grandmother's cakes or sweet breads. I was probably trying to steal her Klim milk powder or the sugar she buried there also, as if it were not the sole ambition of children to seek out secrets. She rotated her hiding places of course, but the wardrobe could always be counted on because before we ruined it there was a lock. And she kept the key in her bosom or under her pillow. My grandmother read the bible from that drawer, putting her finger under each word, then tiring, her eyes or her grasp giving out, she placed it in the recess at the head of her bed before falling asleep, some psalm dying on her lips: "The Lord is my rock, and my fortress, and my deliverer; my God, my strength in who I will trust; my buckler, and the horn of my salvation, and my high tower . . ." The psalm was a prohibition to our desire and a sign of her power attached so intimately, so ardently, to the Lord. It was a psalm denoting her territory, the breadth of her command. But when she was asleep we forgot her power. Then the wardrobe drawer was a lure of tablecloth-covered cakes soaked in rum to keep them moist and crumbling shortbreads in tins from away, powdered milk and Ponds pink face powder, dates, chocolates melting to cherry centres in the heat, Andrew liver salts which frothed in the mouth, avocados left in brown paper to ripen. What led me to this book, then, were my senses, my sweet tooth, my hunger, my curiosity, the intrigue, the possibility of outsmarting my grandmother.

The geometry book I only remember as pages of drawings, signs and symbols with thick dense writing which I could not follow, though I remember elaborate structures, a kind of inexplicable intelligence which I knew I would never conquer but felt I ought to. It had lain in the drawer for years as companion to *The Black Napoleon*. But I never got close to it. I have always been bad at geometry.

I cannot recall the day I decided to read the book, but it must have been the day after my uncle said not to touch it.

Then it became as irresistible as the other contents of the drawer. I opened the book, at first leaving the drawer open with the book lying inside, and began to read. Then I took it to my spot behind the house, then to my spot below the bed. After slipping into this book I understood that my uncle must have fallen into its face, too, and he didn't want any more pages torn out. This book filled me with sadness and courage. It burned my skin. I lay asleep on its open face under the bed. It was the book that took me away from the world, from the small intrigues of sugar and milk to the pleasure and desolation of words on a page. For days I lived with these people I found there, hoping and urging and frightened and elated. The book was about the uprising led by Toussaint L'Ouverture against the French on St. Domingue. In it I met a history I was never taught. The history I had been taught began, "In 1492 Christopher Columbus discovered Santo Domingo . . . with his three ships, the Nina, the Pinta and the Santa Maria he discovered the New World." I had been given the first sighting of land by Cristobal Colon as my beginnings. His eyes, his sight, his view, his vindication, his proof, his discovered terrain. These were to be mine. All the moil and hurt proceeding from his view were to the good, evolutionary, a right and just casualty of modernity. Everything was missing from the middle of that story. Empire was at the end. So I had never met Toussaint L'Ouverture until I saw him at the bottom of the wardrobe drawer with the cakes and sugar. Perhaps I also met there things I had never felt before. I did not know about slavery; I had never felt pain over it. In fact I had never felt pain except the kind of pain that children feel, immediate and transient; I had never seen — well, what can one see in eight years or so of living? — suffering. I did not yet know how the world took people like me. I did not know history. The book was a mirror and an ocean.

Dessalines was said, on the pages of this book, to have been voracious in battle, Toussaint a diplomat. When I was twenty-five or so, I would write in a poem, "Toussaint, I loved you as soon as I saw you on that page." I loved his faith, though it betrayed him. But Dessalines' ardour never would. I loved his ferocity. The poem ended, "Dessalines, Dessalines, you were right . . ." This book I had found inhabited me with its terror and revolution. I was eight or so. It was the first "big" book I read to its end. When I was finished, I was made. I had lost innocence and acquired knowledge. I had lost the idea that desire was plain.

I recall the passion I felt for those people fighting the French. I recognized them. I was them. I remember my small chest — my grandmother called it a bird's chest — wracked with apprehension over the outcome. I would continue to hunt down sugar and milk and black fruitcake and cream wafers, certainly, but *The Black Napoleon* and falling into the face of a book were now entwined and indistinguishable in my sensual knowledge. I read the book over and over again, returning to passages. To Toussaint and Dessalines.

The second book I recall, as one only recalls significance — and recollection is happenstance; things leave sufficient impression to break the surface of thousands of thoughts and experiences — the second book I recall is D.H. Lawrence's *Lady Chatterley's Lover*. This book began as a rumour at twelve or thirteen, a rumour in a girls' high school about a forbidden book. Forbidden because there were "good" parts about explicit sex. When we got hold of the book it was all we could do to keep it secret from the teachers. So amazing and unvarnished were its descriptions that our own language became secretive, even unspoken. I have not read it since. The truth is, I do not remember the book at all. I remember only a gardener (gamekeeper, gatekeeper?), a lady, a kind of anxiety, a kind of exquisite agony I looked forward to having some day. The book had a red cover. It was poured over and crushed. The pages with the good stuff were creased. I remember reading quickly. I remember, too, a feeling of being older, of having read it. Worldly. As if I had been let into another skin, a woman's, a man's. And also, another country's. But I also felt burdened, as if I knew some thing that I should not. Some thing that had changed me into the girl who had read *Lady Chatterley's Lover*, different from the girl who had not read it a moment ago. And I don't think that I read it all. So ravishing were the book's contents that I think each of us only had the chance to read certain paragraphs, hastily. Perhaps different paragraphs, perhaps different stresses for the words of particular sentences. We read quickly, looking up after every line to see if we were in danger of being found out. Our eyes probably landed on completely different places on the page when we looked back. We could not betray each other, or we would lose the possibility of ever knowing the good parts. We only had the one copy. We covered it in brown paper, I think, as my grandmother had covered the avocados, to ripen. We rationed it, keeping only so many paragraphs apiece, so many lines. I read holding my breath, the narrative interpolated into the humid air of a going-home-after-school afternoon. A not-watching-where-you-are-going stumbling, perhaps falling afternoon.

I like to think of us now, eight or so women then girls, each in a different part of the world, each in possession of a different paragraph of *Lady Chatterley's Lover*, a different line now perhaps interrupted, intercut by how we chose to live our lives, how we chose to interpret Lawrence.

I do not know among us who identified with the lady and who with the gamekeeper. The book's gendering could not have been seamless. No book's gendering can be, ultimately, since a book asks us to embody, which at once takes us across borders of all kinds. Or does it dispel borders altogether? Anyway, some of us were him and some of us were her. She seemed light, limnal; he seemed dark, brooding consciousness. This paradigm of the canon was a conflict for us. We were she and he — female, and darkly brooding, becoming the consciousness of the book. Both the possibilities and the constraints of enactment existed within the borderless territory of the book. We were beckoned by some familiarity with her in us, we were willing, eager, to be her. Yet at the same moment of reading her we saw in ourselves the "not-her." She was an ideal of a society which stood in powerful relation to ours. The conversation going on in the book was one about culture, class, technology, and sexuality. It was the same conversation going on in our lives and it was the same conversation going on between the place where the book lived and the place where we lived. This conflict was not fully charged in us yet, or at least it operated as a doubleness. So we wanted to be her, we wanted to be them, we wanted to be there. Yet we recognized the cleavage, the primitive in his cottage at the bottom of the garden, modernity attracted and repelled by him. We were him. We, on an island at the bottom of the New World, we too were representations of the primitive.

The book had begun outside of the book in the rumour. We had begun outside of the book also, the colonial consciousness, the female consciousness. And the curious. When we entered the book, entering for the purposes of identifying and enacting, we were flung apart. We disintegrated, we abstracted. We emerged having reconstructed the novel into a more complex, more fluid sense of desire.

These two books gave me a refractory hunger. Their register and compass led me to all other books.

My uncle let me keep *The Black Napoleon*. It became my book. I do not recall sharing it with my sisters or my cousins or my friends. That time I tried to run away from home at fourteen I tied a belt around it along with the rest of my books, going I don't know where. No clothes, no shoes, just books and three dollars. I could not take *Lady Chatterley's Lover*; I did not have it all. I only had a few lines shared with a few girls.

Books leave gestures in the body; a certain way of moving, of turning, a certain closing of the eyes, a way of leaving, hesitations. Books leave certain sounds, a certain pacing; mostly they leave the elusive, which is all the story. They leave much more than the words. Words can be thrown together. It is their order and when they catch you — their time. These first two books shaped me. And I suspect that I have been writing these two books ever since, recalling and reimagining them. I had been seduced by them. The fact is, I remember them only in my body. I cannot quote a single line from them, and I have not ever felt the need to return to them physically, though I know that I always return to them as I write. The emotions they spoke of were perhaps contradictory to what one might simplistically call desire. But desire is disclosed as a complex. There is a range of experience within the space which is called desire. Toussaint and Dessalines embodied faith and ferocity, different constructs which amplified my sense of desire. The lady and the gamekeeper embodied dissonances of the physical body, the racial body and the gendered body. The canonical locations of light and dark, male, female, master, slave were broken or interrupted in both books. Desire's province widened to the flying pieces, their occasional collection into a movement or a colour or a sigh, ever shifting, ever reimagined.

Writing is an act of desire, as is reading. Why does someone enclose a set of apprehensions within a book? Why does someone else open that book if not because of the act of wanting to be wanted, to be understood, to be seen, to be loved?

And desire is also an act of reading, of translation. The poet Joy Harjo writes, "Nearly everyone had left that bar in the middle of winter except the/ hardcore. It was the coldest night of the year, every place shut down, but/ not us. Of course we noticed when she came in. We were Indian ruins. She/ was the end of beauty."

Desire, too, is the discovery of beauty as miraculous. Desire in the face of ruin. How in these lines there is such wreckage and that too is beauty, how in those lines there is such clear-eyed dread, such deeply mocking knowledge, and that too is desire. How those lines read beauty and desire into any given night, in any place, trailer park wasteland, rural rum shop, shebeen, sports bar, speakeasy, piss-and-beer-reeking dive, beauty walks in. On any given night, even with history against you in any hardscrabble place, beauty walks in. The ruin of history visited on a people does not wipe out the steadfastness of beauty. Not a naive beauty but a hard one. Beauty, it seems, is constantly made. It is both fortunate and unfortunate. Surprising.

For some, to find beauty is to search through ruins. For some of us beauty must be made over and over again out of the sometimes fragile, the sometimes dangerous. To write is to be involved in this act of translation, of succumbing or leaning into another body's idiom. Some years ago a young man surely on his own way to ruin stepped into the street on a square in Amsterdam. The night just approaching, I watched him from a distance well into the night. His figure was in anguish and discomfort; it jangled; it wanted to be and not to be in the square. He was in a kind of despair I have never experienced and experienced then only through his drifting into the street. My despair is private, but his was public and private all at once. His drifting into the street, his slight hesitation — this was beauty. I saw that young man drop into the square like a drop of water into an ocean. That is, I saw his body, his back half-turned toward me, his right leg hovering before stepping off the curb. My eyes followed his yellow-clad body — or it seemed to be yellow in that dark street. The square had a way of darkening with secrets, so the light was yellow, his figure was yellow. That was beauty, his anguish was beauty — his leg stopping, his face whipping round in search of someone, yet his disinterest somehow in people, the glaze to his eyes, yet their sharpness in seeking out the thing, the someone he was after — all was beauty. He was someone in his own gesture, the thing that writers envy. It is clever and cold, edgy, and it belonged to him. To desire then, to read and translate, may also be to envy, to want to become. What is it that I wanted to pour myself into — his grief, his cold sweat, his life uncertain of its next step? And I wanted to do it only for the moment it took to put it on a page, to feel its texture, and then to run back quickly to my uncomplicated hotel room and my as-yet-uncomplicated page. To desire may also be to complicate.

I want to say something else about desire. I really do not know what it is. I experience something which, sometimes, if I pull it apart, I cannot make reason of. The word seems to me to fall apart under the pull and drag of its commodified shapes, under the weight of our artifice and our conceit. It is sometimes impossible to tell what is real from what is manufactured. We live in a world filled with commodified images of desire. Desire clings to widgets, chairs, fridges, cars, perfumes, shoes, jackets, golf clubs, basketballs, telephones, water, soap powder, houses, neighbourhoods. Even god. It clings to an endless list of objects. It clings to the face of television sets and movie screens. It is glaciered in assigned objects, it is petrified in repetitive clichéd gestures. Their repetition is tedious, the look and sound of them tedious. We become the repetition despite our best efforts. We become numb. And though against the impressive strength of this I can't hope to say all that desire might be, I wanted to talk about it not as it is sold to us but as one collects it, piece by piece, proceeding through a life. I wanted to say that life, if we are lucky, is a collection of aesthetic experiences as it is a collection of practical experiences, which may be one and the same sometimes, and which if we are lucky we make a sense of. Making sense may be what desire is. Or, putting the senses back together.

## Maps

In 14th century Songhay books were sold for more money than other goods. At Jenne, gold, ivory, skins, pepper and rubber were exchanged for cloth, salt, glass beads, iron, copper and manuscripts.

Ezio Bassani, in *Circa 1492*

## Museums

This novel begins in a museum. A small white museum which once housed eighteenth-century British colonial military. It is a small building with two floors, wooden and creaky. It has the smell of all colonial buildings, a yellow handwritten papery mustiness which reminds one of khaki breeches, white sea-island cotton shirts, endless reams of paper, carbon duplicates, and ink wells. It reminds one of interminable waiting. You arrive at the small white museum by climbing or driving up the steepest hill in the town. Up this hill was once a fort. Fort King George. Laid down around 1783, this fort was named for George III of England. You come past the once regiment buildings, and the once domed iron jailhouse which rests in one side of the hill. You imagine eighteenth- and nineteenth-century prisoners baking in this iron prison atop this highest of peaks in the town.

On the other side of the narrow road up the hill are flamboyant trees, ranging, graceful, and red. As you crest the hill, there is the ocean, the Atlantic, and there a fresh wide breeze relieving the deep flush of heat. From atop this hill you can see over the whole town. Huge black cannons overlook the ocean, the harbour, and the town's perimeter. If you look right, if your eyes could round the point, you would see the Atlantic and the Caribbean in a wet blue embrace. If you come here at night you will surprise lovers, naked or clothing askew, groping hurriedly or dangerously languorous, draped against the black gleaming cannons of George III. At night it is cool and breezy here, and dark; in the daytime it is stark and chalk white and hot, except for the ever blue sky and the flame trees — at their torrid best in the dry season. This book begins in the small white stone museum to the left of the cannons. As you enter there is the sound of a ceiling fan, whirring somewhere in an office upstairs. A clerk asks you apologetically for five TT dollars and ushers you in. On the first floor are bones, shells, stones, small carvings, arrowheads, broken amulets of the first peoples who inhabited this island. It strikes me that on the first floor of all our consciousness, all our imaginations in the Americas, there are these particular bones, shells carvings, arrowheads, broken amulets of the first peoples who inhabited this New World. The legends on the glass cabinet seem unsure of dates, names; there is not enough money to investigate details, the curator says. To enhance the exhibit the curator has installed a carved boat from Guyana or Surinam, the kind these peoples must have used two or three thousand years ago to make the trip by water to this island from the South American continent. Already this novel is about forgetting. Several millennia have been consumed in the airless small room of this exhibit. This small wreckage of broken stones, bones, and carvings strewn in a glass case without classification or dating is what is left of millions of journeys, millions of songs, millions of daily acts, millions of memories that no one remembers.

On this hill with its wide sumptuous view of black glittering water at night, its blue forever in the daytime, this museum's vain attempt at recollection is visited by few. Guilt makes me want to stop longer at the glass cabinet even though it is possible to see all there is here in a matter of minutes. Fear of disrespect to something quite old makes me linger but then sheepishly move on. Out of the corner of my eye I see a wicker sack where bitter cassava was drained of its poison; I see an arrow whose head might have been tarred with woorara. I make a note without even knowing why and I walk away.

Glancing away from the glass cabinet's debris is looking away from history as well as being filled, uneasily, with history. Moving away is escaping it and this novel is escaping as well as succumbing. Edouard Glissant, the Martiniquan critic, says, "History is destined to be pleasure or distress . . . is capable of quarrying deep within us, as a consciousness or the emergence of a consciousness, as a neurosis and a contraction of the self." This novel begins as I move to the staircase to the second floor. The staircase creaks before my weight has time to rest on it, it creaks from the thought of another body weighing it down, inquiring. The feeling that I carry from the glass cabinet to the stairs is already in the novel — discomfort. This novel will not breath on those bones; if it does it will be brief like the brief rain the Caribs disappear into on this work's second page, it will be brief and therefore mythic. Those bones warn me that everything after I have made up, I have invented in absence.

Moving up the staircase to the next rooms of the museum where this novel begins, I am distressed, in Glissant's sense, and also curious, which is pleasure. The rooms above contain maps, the works of eighteenth-century cartographers growing more and more skilled at forgetting as time passed, maps, ascertaining courses and distances, astronomic observations made on the land, latitudes taken at sea, soundings of banks and harbours and bays, bearings for ships. These cartographers, they were artists and poets. They were dreamers and imaginers as surely as I. On a *Chart of The Antilles, or Charibbee, or, Caribs Islands with the Virgin Isles* by Louis De La Rochette, drawn and published in 1784, there are angels, or cherubs, mouths pursed, blowing the trade winds west on the Atlantic. You must remember this is one point of the middle passage. People are to be lost here, drowned here; people are to be sold, backs and hearts broken; those cherubs, their sweet lips pursed, blow a rough trade. Only an artist could render an angel here. Wonderful wind roses adorn these maps, ships under full sail; cartouches of sovereigns, great explorers, and welcoming nubile natives.

Thomas Jefferys, geographer to the king, George III, writes, in a strangely elegant prose, his observations of this island with the small museum and the cabinet of bones:

> *The currents near Tobago are very strong and uncertain efpecially between this island and Trinidad. At the full and change of the moon the sea will rise four feet perpendicular. The North east trades blow all year round. The numerical figures denote e/y depth of water in fathoms where e/y anchors are exprefsed it is good anchorage Man-o-War Bay, Courland, Sandy Point and King's Bay are for vessels of the largest size. Tyrrel's Bay, Bloody Bay,*

*Parlatuviers Bay at Englishman's Bay, Castara Bay and
La Guira's Bay have safe anchorage for vefsels of 150 tuns
or under. Halifax Bay is very safe and snug for ships
under 250 Tuns but there is a shoal in e/y middle of e/y
entrance that makes a Pilot necessary. If you make Tobago
toward evening and are afraid of running in with it you
must not by any means lay to but fstand to e/y southward
under an easy sail otherwise e/y current which always sets
to e/y North west or north east will probably occasion your
lofsing sight of the island and if it set north west would
perhaps carry you so far to e/y leeward that you should not
be able to fetch it again. Vefsels sailing from e/y eastward
for e/y south side of e/y island, must keep well to e/y southward, otherwise the current round Little Tobago which
run always to e/y North west will sweep them away to e/y
northwest. To the South west there is nothing to fear, till
you come to Courland Bay but what shows itself, except
Chesterfield rocks . . .*

This novel begins most assuredly here in this sublime narrative. I am stunned as I read it with its lisping s's, I am fasci-
nated by its unintended irony, I am in love with its cadence;
what movement in, "[Do] not by any means lay to but stand
to under an easy sail." I am envious the way it speaks so
gently to its readers, so surely. Its authority in apprehend-
ing what others cannot apprehend, its command of the

geography of the oceans — How wilting! How majestic! This gorgeous prose dissembles, it obstructs our view of its real directions, it alludes, it masks. But it points, it says, there, that is where you land the ships bringing slaves to this island. It says that it is possible to do this and still maintain gifts of erudition, or intelligence, even playfulness. Language is so wonderful, so deceitful. Which is why 230 years later I wrench it from his pen, I tear it from the wall of this museum, I cut it into pieces — one piece for the title of this novel, *At the Full and Change of the Moon*, and the rest I give to my Kamena, who escapes the slave plantation at Mon Chagrin in this novel and who in this novel is searching for Terre Bouillante, a maroonage; who is searching in this novel for a place he will never find. He must instead take Bola, the child of a woman named Marie Ursule, a woman who at the beginning of this novel is about to commit suicide; he must take this child Bola and care for her until she can make generations who will inhabit our century. He never finds what he is looking and longing for, it eludes him, it dissembles, all of his directions lead him nowhere. His observations are unearthly. . .

Kamena's unending and, as history will confirm, inevitably futile search for a homeland is the mirror of the book's later generations — their dispersal, their scatterings to the extreme and remote corners of the world: Amsterdam, New

York, Toronto. Their distraction and flights resound in him and back to him. It is their condition of being. This is what they give all cities; they inhabit temporariness, elsewhere — thinking of something they cannot remember but thinking furiously. The journey is the destination.

I use Jefferys' observations not as he had, to show the way to slavery, but to sail my characters into the late twentieth century. The unholy paradox of it does not escape me, I cannot undo Jefferys' words, which might look like simple directions to some; I cannot unhappen history and neither can my characters. When asked, as in Derek Walcott's poem, "Where are your monuments, your battles, martyrs?/ Where your tribal memory?" my characters answer as in that poem, "Sirs,/ in that grey vault. The sea. The sea/ has locked them up." My characters can only tear into pieces, both history and Jefferys' observations, they can only deliberately misplace directions and misread observations. They can take north for south, west for east. Anywhere they live is remote. They can in the end impugn the whole theory of directions. They inhabit everywhere, mostly the metropoles of North America and Europe. Their lives take any direction at any moment.

In this museum are records, books, lists, names of the enslaved and their age, sex, and physical condition. This novel begins in the jumble of names I've read. I look down each list, I try to imagine someone writing these lists. Would they have written them down at the beginning of the crop, at the end of the crop, or would they have kept a running record? Would they have had a cup of tea before going to the job or would they have stopped in the middle, gone home to have an afternoon nap, and returned thinking what a nuisance paperwork was? Or would this someone have written these names quite happily, with flourish in the wrist, congratulating himself or herself on the good condition and quantity of their livestock. I cannot help wondering at the personal while reading these lists. What did May, girl, ten, sickly, look like? Or Alfred, man, twenty (?), good health? There are no ruins of slave houses on this island. Their lodgings were so poorly made, so transient, nothing is left of that. Perhaps that is all to the good. Forgetting is a crucial condition of living with any peace. But the records of what and how are in the living, in our habits, our tastes, our styles — a sweet tooth, a love of starchy foods, a sudden hatred of fields, a desire for big cities, an insistent need for loud colours, beautiful shoes, excesses of all kinds whether we can afford them or not.

I scour this museum to understand what is already written in this novel, what is already written in this novel writing itself. I scour many museums. In these museums are signs of exits from the Door of No Return. In another museum, on another island, I find an eighteenth-century prison dress once worn by a woman who was a slave. It is hanging on an iron mannequin in a dank room in the belly of another eighteenth-century fort. It is stiff, mildewed, and for one moment I wonder why, why have they kept this since there seems to be no reason in the assortment of items here, sugar boiling coppers of various sizes, saddles, ladles . . . Why this dress? A dour dress, as any prison dress might be in any century, doubtless, but a dress as if waiting for this novel to inhabit it, to give it life. Writers, I know, are egotistical sad beings but this dress was waiting for me, it was waiting for the fiction of my Marie Ursule to inhabit it. Looking at this dress I felt a chill, a determination which I could never have myself; I could not be that single-minded or have that much conviction or perhaps that much love to last several centuries to inhabit a novel. The memory of this dress arrives one night along with a memory of V.S. Naipaul's *The Loss of Eldorado: A History*. In it he tells of a woman, Thisbe, who was a slave and the main suspect in a mass death by poisoning on a plantation. After being on trial for several months and tortured throughout, she was sentenced to death. Thisbe was "hanged, her body mutilated and burnt and her head spiked on a pole. At her hanging she was reported to have said, 'This is but a drink of water to what I have already suffered.'" My character, named Marie Ursule, wakes up on the first morning of the novel heading for that dour mildewed prison dress and those words which Naipaul snatched from history and which I receive from him, gratefully. And the novel begins, "Marie Ursule woke up the morning, knowing what morning it was and that it might be her last."

This novel begins in a memoir of Père Labat, a French priest who went to Martinique and the French colonies in the seventeenth century. There, in cheery recollections of his adventures and life among the colonists, I find two Ursuline nuns, Mère Marguerite de St-Joseph and Soeur de Clemy. They have a convent, two novices, a plantation, and nineteen slaves. They are very good businesswomen because, according to Père Labat, when they die without consecrating their novices into nuns, the Jesuit priests claim their estate. Père Labat's sanguine account of all this, his own travels and business dealings, the ways of planters, the workings of capital machines, his fascination with and disdain for the rituals of the indigenous peoples, his enthusiasm for the whole matter of colonizing, makes you understand just how plain and ordinary this all was, how commonplace and regular — and not in the least bit extraordinary — brutality and exploitation are. And how god is tied up in it up to his neck. The nuns sparkle in Père Labat's narrative even though he only deals with them briefly. I imagine them moving calmly and ghostly among the teeming crowds at the docks in Marseille in 1680 or so, their habits dragging on the ground, their barrels or bundles carried by the novices, making passage on the ship called *Tranquille*. They are going to the colonies to convert savages. When I meet them in Père Labat's narrative I write them into ever. In the novel they are hundreds of years old. They hover over the work.

This novel flees from that century. It does all it can do to make distance between itself and those catastrophes — Marie Ursule, the nuns, the cartographers. It makes haste through the hurricane of 1875, when a boy is swept away from all his might-have-beens. Another boy goes off to the First World War only to find himself digging latrines. One woman has a sudden and great lust for the glint of gold things and fine cloth. The descendants of those early narratives cross to the mainland of South America, step back onto the archipelago time and again, unknown and known to each other, aware and unaware of their history. Some make their way by water and guile all the way to North America and Europe. That eighteenth-century cartographer's theory of directions is unravelling in this novel. By the end of the twentieth century what the lines on Jefferys' map have conspired to hold in has burst out. What he had not counted on was Marie Ursule, but Marie Ursule had counted on nothing, just whim, a decision to let her child Bola escape with Kamena. Counting on her own theory, the theory of nothing, she had opened up the world. In every city in the Old World are Marie Ursule's New World wanderers real and chimeric.

Museums; museums are not only enclosures of and for the dead. They are also wide vistas and dark alleyways, car rides across the backs of cities and bodies wrapped in cold coats. This novel begins with the living in Dam Square, Amsterdam, 1992.

Truthfully, this novel begins because I have lost my luggage on my way to Amsterdam. In Glasgow I search and search for my suitcase until the plane to Amsterdam is about to leave. I board my flight to Schiphol feeling somewhat bereft. I have the clothes on my back. I am in Europe with only the clothes on my back but I have my passport and my money and thank goodness the volume of poetry I am to read from the following night. My most horrible nightmare will not come true. The nightmare where I am at a poetry reading and I discover that I have forgotten my book at home and I cannot remember a single line of my poetry. My luggage . . . to be without luggage. I wonder if this is how they felt in that other century, no familiar thing which would suggest that you decided to travel, you have a destination, a place where you will land and open your suitcase and put your things away and then go outside and see what is there. You will be a traveller, you will look at your surroundings as a place to discover, you will decide what to eat, who to speak with, where to sleep. You will expect recognition and interest, even fellowship.

I land at Schiphol, Amsterdam, without my luggage. Unlike Jefferys. I have no compass. Nor do I have a dispensation from a king to map a shoreline or, in my case, a city. Anyway, it is 1992, and travel is now different though sometimes the same. I am a traveller but I do not travel to the New World (as travellers do today) to encounter a shaman who will take me to my inner soul, a shaman whom I will consume with the greed of a Coca-Cola drinker, a shaman who will disappoint me eventually and inevitably since in the grand narrative the outcome of such encounters must confirm the fallibility of the shaman's magic and the infallibility of my Coca-Cola. I travel to the Old World to be . . . well . . . to be an exotic. I am not a traveller then; I am an exotic in the best of circumstances, an out-of-place nuisance in the worst. The mythology is already known, already in place, my travelogues will not be sent home to make maps for science and commerce. I cannot reflect, question, demonize, or assimilate the monuments of Europe. I have no centre which domesticates the periphery. I do not even have my own luggage. I do not know Amsterdam; I do not have a map. The ex-policeman concierge who told me that he had been to Canada to a police convention gestures in the direction of a flea market where I might find some second-hand clothes to wear. I should not be coy here, there is no prison dress waiting for me, only haunting me. It will take a day or two to get my luggage. It has apparently gone to New York. Following the ex-policeman's directions I wander over to the flea market, buy a shirt, then wander about other streets looking for clothing stores.

I walk along the canal, getting lost, losing my bearings, until something else takes my eyes, a window. A woman is in the window, she is standing next to a table, she looks at ease. I say to myself, "Oh, of course there are Black people here, Curacao, Surinam, the Dutch West Indies." I stare at her; she stares back until I feel that I am intruding. I miss my step like a gazing child. When I look up there is another window with another woman, then another, then another. It dawns on me slowly as history, "Oh!" How artless of me. Oh yes, it's Amsterdam. I am struck by the fact that all the scenes in the windows are domestic. My character Maya stares at me impatiently, waiting for me to recognize her, then as if having no time with my innocence she goes about her business. This window and this woman, the one sitting so casually, find their way into the novel.

Eduardo Galeano writes in *Walking Words*, "I'm alone in a foreign city, and I don't know anyone, nor do I understand the language. But suddenly someone shines in the middle of the crowd, shining suddenly like a word lost on the page or any patch of grass on the skin of the earth." In Dam Square I spot my character Adrian. It is night; he is walking busily back and forth in a jerky walk. He is wiping sweat from his face with a distracted hand. His body is light and wind-bent though there is no wind. He gathers his coat up around his ears though it is summer. But he is cold from something missing in his veins. He is trembling. With my usual preciousness at first I do not catch the play for some minutes. Then he shines. That is Kamena's boy, the boy lost to directions. Then I am sad on Dam Square. All the way here, all the way here to look so dry faced on Dam Square. I feel like sitting there, right there beneath the statue covered in pigeon waste, I feel like sitting there and crying, I feel bereft. I feel abandoned by Marie Ursule to city squares and windows and public places where I am on display and must make a display, like exotica. I feel marooned like Kamena. Marooned now in outposts and suburbs and street corners anywhere in the world. I am adrift, spilled out, with Adrian and Maya at the end of this century in any city all over the world with nothing as certain as Marie Ursule coming. We are all abandoned, all scattered in Marie Ursule's hopelessness and her skill.

This novel doesn't begin because of any of this. It begins because I am a writer. I like the way a word can bloom a whole other set of words, and I like the gesture of an arm on a street corner or in a church. I like the faint whiff of perfume, a hip-shotted walk, a trail of cloth, dappling light off a tree through a curtain at a window, strong coffee artichoke hearts and dry white wine. The novel begins because I am sitting in a two-storey pine house in the middle of winter in Burnt River drinking coffee, and a spider is figuring out how to catch the flies buzzing on the windowpane and by this time I have no other skill so I begin to write.

*Maps*

An oral ruttier is a long poem containing navigational instructions which sailors learned by heart and recited from memory. The poem contained the routes and tides, the stars and maybe the taste and flavour of the waters, the coolness, the saltiness; all for finding one's way at sea. Perhaps, too, the reflection and texture of the sea bed, also the sight of birds, the direction of their flight. This and an instrument called a Kamal which measured the altitude of stars from the horizon.

## Ruttier for the Marooned in the Diaspora

Marooned, tenantless, deserted. Desolation castaway, abandoned in the world. They was, is, wandered, wanders as spirits who dead cut, banished, seclude, refuse, shut the door, derelict, relinquished, apart. More words she has left them. Cast behind. From time to time they sit on someone's bed or speak to someone in the ear and that is why someone steps out of rhythm; that is why someone drinks liquor or trips or shuts or opens a door out of nowhere. All unavailable to themselves, open to the world, cut in air. They disinherit answers. They owe, own nothing. They whisper every so often and hear their own music in churches, restaurants, hallways, all paths, between fingers and lips, between cars and precipices, and the weight of themselves in doorways, on the legs of true hipsters, guitars and bones for soup, veins.

And it doesn't matter where in the world, this spirit is no citizen, no national, no one who is christened, no sex, this spirit is washed of all this lading, bag and baggage, jhaji bundle, georgie bindle, lock stock, knapsack, and barrel, and only holds its own weight which is nothing, which is memoryless and tough with remembrances, heavy with lightness, aching with grins. They wander as if they have no century, as if they can bound time, as if they can sit in a café in Brugge just as soon as smoke grass in Tucson, Arizona, and chew coca in the high Andes for coldness.

Pays for everything this one, hitchhikes, dies in car accidents, dresses in Hugo Boss and sings ballads in Catholic churches, underwater rum shops. This is a high-wire spirit laden with anchors coming in to land, devoluting heirlooms, parcels, movable of nips, cuts, open secrets of foundlings, babes, ignitions, strips of water, cupfuls of land, real estates of ocean floors and steaming asphalt streets, meat of trees and lemons, bites of Communion bread and chunks of sky, subdivisions of stories.

These spirits are tenants of nothing jointly, temporary inheritors of pages 276 and 277 of an old paleology. They sometimes hold a life like a meeting in a detention camp, like a settlement without a stone or stick, like dirty shelves, like a gag in the mouth. Their dry goods are all eaten up already and their hunger is tenacious. This spirit doubling and quadrupling, resuming, skipping stairs and breathing elevators is possessed with uncommunicated undone plots; consignments of compasses whose directions tilt, skid off known maps, details skitter off like crabs. This spirit abandoned by all mothers, fathers, all known progenitors, rents rooms that disappear in its slate stone wise faces. These people un-people, de-people until they jump overboard, hijack buildings and planes. They disinhabit unvisited walls. They unfriend friends in rye and beer and homemade wine and forties.

She undwells solitudes, liquors' wildernesses. This drunk says anything, cast away in his foot ship, retired from the world. This whisperer, sprawler, mincer, deaconess, soldier is marooning, is hungering, is unknowing. This one in the suit is a litigant in another hearing gone in the world. This spirit inhaling cigarettes is a chain along a thousand glistening moss harbours and spends nights brooding and days brooding and afternoons watching the sea even at places with no harbours and no sea. This one is gone, cast off and wandering wilfully. This is intention as well as throwaway. This is deliberate and left. Slipstream and sailing. Deluge. These wander anywhere, clipping shirt-tails and hems and buying shoes and vomiting. These shake with dispossession and bargain, then change their minds. They get trapped in houses one minute, just as anybody can, and the next they break doorways and sit in company mixing up the talk with crude honesty and lies. Whatever is offered or ceded is not the thing, not enough, cannot grant their easement, passports to unknowing everything.

This spirit's only conveyance is each morning, breath, departures of any kind, tapers, sheets of anything, paper, cloth, rain, ice, spittle, glass. It likes blue and fireflies. Its face is limpid. It has the shakes, which is how it rests and rests cutting oval shells of borders with jagged smooth turns. It is an oyster leaving pearl. These spirits have lived in any given year following the disaster, in any given place. They have visited shutters and doors and thermal glass windows looking for themselves. They are a prism of endless shimmering colour. If you sit with them they burn and blister. They are bony with hope, muscular with grief possession.

Marooned on salted highways, in high grass, on lumpy beds, in squares with lights, in knowledge plantations and cunning bridges grasping two cities at the same time. Marooned in the mouth where things escape before they are said, are useless before they are given or echo. Marooned in realms of drift, massacres of doubt, implications. Marooned where the body burns with longing for everything and nothing, where it circles unable to escape a single century; tenements and restagings of alien, new landings. Marooned in outcropping, up-crops of cities already abandoned for outposts in suburbs. Deserted in the fragility of concrete rooms, the chalked clammy dust of dry walls, the rot of sewer pipes and the blanket of city grates.

Marooned in music, dark nightclubs of weeping, in never-sufficient verses, uncommunicated sentences, strict tears, in copper throats. Where days are prisons this spirit is a tenant.

She moves along incognito on foot, retreating into unknowing, retreating into always orphanages, dew light, paradise, eclipses, bruised skies, atomic stars, an undeviating ever.

So if now and then they slump on beds in exhaustion it is hallowed pain. If they sink in the ear it is subversions that change their minds even before they are deployed, unexpected architectures of ambivalent longing, cargoes of wilderness. It is their solitudes' wet desolations. If they finger a string across a piece of wood and a tremolo attacks a room, toccata erupt, coloratura saturate the walls, it is their lost and found dereliction. If virtuosity eludes them, relinquishes them, cast away to themselves only, gaping limbs and topographies, it is just as much spiritoso, madrigal, mute chirping, ululating twilight unvisiting.

It is now and she, they whisper in Walkmans, in cities' streets with two million people gazing at advertisements. It is now and he, they run his fingers over a moustache flicking frost away, breathing mist like a horse. Cities and public squares and public places corral their gifts of imagined suns and imagined families, where they would have been and who they might have been and when. Cities make them pause and wonder at what they might have thought had it been ever, and had it been dew light and had it been some other shore, and had it been time in their own time when now they are out of step with themselves as spirits are. Electric lights and neon and cars' metal humming convince them of cultivated gateways and generations of water, of necessities they cannot put back together. Their coherence is incoherence, provocations of scars and knives and paradise, of tumbling wooden rivers and liquid hills.


## Maps

There is an old man who walks back and forth at Shuter and Parliament. He has all his belongings in a bag on his back and another in his hand. Every time I pass by, year in, year out, he is pacing, pacing back and forth. The story goes that many years ago he used to live with his daughter, who struggled to keep him with her but eventually had to give up. He had Alzheimer's disease. His daughter finally and reluctantly brought him to the mission to stay, as she could no longer care for him. He, not understanding that he now lives at the mission, paces back and forth with all his belongings in readiness, waiting for his daughter to return and take him home.

*Maps*

It is not a question of rootlessness but of the miracle
of roots, the miracle of a dialogue with eclipsed selves
which appearances may deny us or into which they
may lead us.

Wilson Harris

1

Vancouver, 2000. Waiting for the bus at Granville and
Robson. The bus arrives. A Black man is driving it. This city
has few Black people. So few that when they meet on the
street they nod to each other in surprise, perhaps delight,
certainly some odd recognition. Two stops along a Salish
woman gets on. She asks the driver for directions — if she
is on the right bus, if she is headed in the right direction,
where she is situated, how much does the fare cost . . .

This road along which the bus travels may have been a path
hundreds of years ago. This jutting of land through which
this path travels has lost its true name. It is now surrounded
by English Bay, False Creek, and Burrard Inlet. And Granville
Street, whose sure name has vanished, once was or was not a
path through. That woman asking directions might have
known these names several hundred years ago. Today when
she enters the bus she is lost. She looks into the face of

another, a man who surely must be lost, too, but who knows the way newly mapped, superimposed on this piece of land; she asks this man the way and sits down. The man driving the bus is driving across a path which is only the latest redrawing of old paths. He is not from here. Where he is from is indescribable and equally vanished from his memory or the memory of anyone he may remember. He is here most recently perhaps from Regina, Saskatchewan, where his mother arrived with her new husband from Toronto, and before that Chicago and still again Bridgetown. And then again the Door of No Return, El Mina or Gorée Island, somewhere along the west coast of the continent, somewhere safe and deep enough to be a harbour and a door to nothing. This driver knows some paths that are unrecoverable even to himself. He is the driver of lost paths. And here he is telling the Salish woman where to go. The woman from this land walks as one blindfolded, no promontory or dip of water is recognizable. She has not been careless, no. No, she has tried to remember, she has an inkling, but certain disasters have occurred and the street, the path in her mind, is all rubble, so she asks the driver through lost paths to conduct her through her own country. So the driver through lost maps tells the woman of a lost country her way and the price she should pay, which seems little enough — $1.50 — to find your way. The woman with no country pays and sits down. The man with no country drives on.

It is only the Granville bus, surely. But a bus where a ragged mirage of histories comes into a momentary realization.

I am sitting on the bus driving along Granville with a friend. She and I observe this transaction. We just made a similar one ourselves with the bus driver of lost paths. The bus is full, but there are really only four of us on it. The driver through lost paths stops and lets someone on and someone off, people who don't realize that the bus is empty but for the four of us. The four of us pause at these intrusions, but we go on. We have perfected something — each of us something different. One drives through lost paths, one asks the way redundantly, one floats and looks, one looks and floats — all marvel at their ability to learn and forget the way of lost maps. We all feign ignorance at the rupture in mind and body, in place, in time. We all feel it.

2

I am going to Seattle. I have just crossed the Winnebago Indian Reservation and the White Earth Indian Reservation. It is not my fault that I notice the earth is scarred. Crow Indian Reservation, Little Belt Mountain, Big Baldy Mountain, Custer's Battlefield Monument, Yakima Indian Reservation. This continent's ancestry is beneath this aircraft.

I will talk in a room in Seattle about another ancestry, of which I have none.

## 3

It was said in my family that my grandfather was part Carib. The parts of my grandfather which were part Carib were his cheekbones, which were high, not in an African-high way but in a square flat way — a Carib-high way. Then there was the tawny hue sometimes visible under the dark brown of his skin. Then the occasional straightness of regions of hair on his head. The rest of my grandfather, his height, the remaining territories of his hair, the dominant colour of his skin, the majority of him, was African. There were, too, indefinite parts of him which either hegemony could claim. But there was no war, there never had been, both had settled calmly in my grandfather. They shared a common history. The Carib part grateful for its small survival in my grandfather's face. A survival once recorded in a letter by Pero Vaz de Caminha to Dom Manuel I of Portugal as "bestial people, with little knowledge . . . they are like birds or mountain animals . . . brown men all nude with nothing to cover their shameful parts." The African part of my grandfather carried him as a courtesy and a welcome obligation and perhaps also in gratitude himself for sharing with him the knowledge of the islands. My grandfather was an agriculturist.

My grandfather came from a country which was devastated by a volcano. This was the island where my grandfather collected the Carib in him. He left when he was a boy. Perhaps the Carib in him, after 2000 years of knowing islands, felt the tremors of Montserrat and propelled my grandfather to a boat heading south a lifetime earlier. My grandfather came from a people whose name he could not remember. His forgetting was understandable; after all, when he was born the Door of No Return was hardly closed, forgetting was urgent.

## 4

I've seen that castle in photographs, the one at Elmina. I've seen it from the angle of the sea, whitewashed and sprawling. There are photographs of what look like narrow low-ceilinged corridors; bats hang in these corridors' dark reaches. I know that if I go to that place I will be destroyed. Its photographs take my breath away. Places like this are dotted along the west coast of Africa. These places became known as the Gate of No Return, the Door of No Return. Does all terror become literary? These are the places that made everyone who went through forget their names. Here, walls ate the skin, footsteps took the mind. My grandfather's forgetting was not personal. It had been passed on to him by many, most especially the one in my family who stepped through the Door of No Return. It was a gift. Forgetting.

The only gift that one, the one bending reluctantly toward the opening, could give.


## 5

To travel without a map, to travel without a way. They did, long ago. That misdirection became the way. After the Door of No Return, a map was only a set of impossibilities, a set of changing locations.


## 6

A map, then, is only a life of conversations about a forgotten list of irretrievable selves.

# Acknowledgements

I am deeply grateful to my editor, Maya Mavjee, for her immense patience and her extraordinary skill. I simply cannot thank her sufficiently for her work here.

I owe much of the information on maps, mapmaking and New World exploration to four texts: *Landmarks of Mapmaking: An Illustrated Survey of Maps and Mapmakers, chosen and displayed by R.V. Tooley; Maps Are Territories,* by David Turnbull; *Great Explorers,* by William Bosman, et al.; and *Circa 1492: Art in the Age of Exploration,* by Jay A. Levenson, et al.

Thank you to Nuzhat Abbas, Ted Chamberlin, Dateje Green, Michael Ondaatje and Jean Pearce for the loan of these and other books, which after two years in some cases I have yet to return. Thanks too to Leslie Saunders and Rinaldo Walcott for many glasses of wine and much reading of the manuscript at various stages. Most deep thanks and praise to Kwame Dawes for his reading, criticism and generous comradeship. Thanks also to my research assistants Charmaine Perkins and Dara Romain. And to the Ruth Wynn Woodward Professorship of the Women's Studies

Department of Simon Fraser University. Without this last, this book could not have been completed.

I am particularly indebted to these remarkable writers: Ezio Bassani, Charles Bricker, Aimé Césaire, J.M. Coetzee, Leonardo da Vinci, Pero Vaz de Caminha, Olaudah Equiano, Eduardo Galeano, Andre Gidé, James Jess Hannon, Wilson Harris, Joy Harjo, Cecil Howard, Thomas Jefferys, D.H. Lawrence, Toni Morrison, Chantal Mouffe, V.S. Naipaul, Pablo Neruda, Jacques Prevert, Jean Rhys, Muriel Rukeyser, David Turnbull, Derek Walcott, and Jack E. White.

# Selected Reading

Bassani, Ezio. from *Circa 1492: Art in the Age of Exploration*, by Jay A. Levenson, et al. Yale, 1992.

Bricker, Charles. *Landmarks of Mapmaking: An Illustrated Survey of Maps and Mapmakers*. Dorset, 1981.

Césaire, Aimé. *Cahier D'Un Retour Au Pays Natal.* Ohio State University Press, 2000.

Coetzee, J.M. *Disgrace.* Viking, 1999.

Equiano, Olaudah. *The African: The Interesting Narrative of the Life of Olaudah Equiano.* X-Press, 1999.

Galeano Eduardo. *Walking Words.* Norton, 1995

Gidé, Andre. *Voyage au Congo et la Retour du Chad.* Knopf, 1929.

Hannon, James Jess. *The Black Napoleon: Toussaint L'Ouverture Liberator of Haiti.* 1st Books Library, 2000.

Howard, Cecil. *West African Explorers.* Oxford University Press. 1951.

Lawrence, D.H. *Lady Chatterley's Lover.* Grove, 1993.

Morrison, Toni. *Paradise.* Knopf, 1998.

Morrison, Toni. *Beloved*. Plume, 1988.

Morrison, Toni. *Song of Solomon.* Plume, 1987

Naipaul, V. S. *The Loss of Eldorado.* Knopf, 1970

Naipaul, V.S. *The Overcrowded Barracoon and Other Articles.* Knopf, 1973

Neruda, Pablo. *Letter to Miguel Otero Silva, in Caracas.* Curbstone Press, 1982.

Prevert, Jacques. *Selections from Paroles.* City Lights, 1958.

Rhys, Jean. *Wide Sargasso Sea.* Norton, 1996.

*Time* Magazine: October 19, 2000.

Turnbull, David. *Maps Are Territories : Science Is an Atlas : A Portfolio of Exhibits.* University of Chicago Press, 1994.

Walcott, Derek. *The Bounty.* Farrar Straus & Giroux, 1997.

White, Jack E. "New York Times," *Time* Magazine: June 7, 1999.

*A note on the author*

Dionne Brand won the Governor General's Award for Poetry and the Trillium Award in 1997 for *Land to Light On*. Her novel, *In Another Place, Not Here*, was shortlisted for the Chapters/Books in Canada First Novel Award and the Trillium Award, and was published in the US and the UK to great acclaim. She lives in Toronto.